DEEP TRAVEL

Deep Travel

At Home in the [Burning] World

A Contemporary Haibun Collection

Dane Cervine

Saddle Road Press

Deep Travel © Dane Cervine, 2024

All rights reserved. No part of this book may be reproduced or transmitted in any form or by any means without written permission of the author.

Saddle Road Press
Ithaca, NY
saddleroadpress.com

Design by Don Mitchell
Cover image (at Barcelona Picasso Museum) by Linda Kittle
Interior images by Dane Cervine and Linda Kittle

ISBN 9798990054349
Library of Congress Control Number: 2024946197

Books by Dane Cervine

The World Is God's Language (Sixteen Rivers Press)
Earth Is a Fickle Dancer (Main Street Rag)
The Gateless Gate – Polishing the Moon Sword (Saddle Road Press)

Contents

Preface	11

The Midwest in Early Spring

Here from California for a Catholic wedding,	17
And what a wedding it was,	18
Between Covington, Kentucky, and Cincinnati,	19
I'd wandered Chicago all day,	20
Linda's last morning in America,	21
The journey west from Chicago to Oakland	22
I relish the single red rose on white tablecloth	23
Meanwhile, carried west in my tiny Amtrak cell,	24
Linda and I both feel this grandparent-season of life	25
Trains are good for reverie.	26
The Amtrak breakfast remains a modest	27
We've been ascending the eastern hills	28
Our train enters northwestern Colorado,	29
Breakfast in the Amtrak dining car	30
Well, the California Zephyr train drama	32

Portugal in May

Surreal—I wake in California texting Linda in Portugal,	35
The trans-Atlantic flight from Denver to Frankfurt,	36
It is my first full day in Santiago,	37
Then, we find the Museum of Pilgrimage & Santiago,	38
After a night of murky dreams, we catch a tour bus	39
On the three-hour bus ride from Santiago to Porto,	40
Writing is my way of walking, I tell Linda	41
We are on pilgrimage together,	42
I travel with my books.	43
Even history museums don't know their own stories.	44
As with my own family history, the further I go back,	45

Spain, just over the Pyrenees, a brash older brother	46
Light rain in Porto, so we are happy to find shelter	47
After the forlorn churches, we walk	48
The rain begins to lightly fall as we wander	49
We head into downtown Porto	50
We cross the Douro River	51
In our Porto flat, a sudden rainstorm	52
Every day, we walk the Rua de Santa Catarina	53
Roaming Porto's riverwalk along the Douro River.	54
We spy a library-museum—the Museu da Cidade	55
This morning, I keep in the spirit of Andalusia	56
We'll travel to Morocco soon, so I sit curbside	57
Holy Toledo indeed!	58
We've another Porto week in this now-familiar apartment	59
In my journal, I sit with Pessoa at the window	60
Woke to warm Porto sun off the balcony.	61
Our Porto cloister at Rua D. João IV, 376,	62
In this lost land of old Andalusia, I read an essay	63
Cloudy Porto skies. The haziness of sleep.	65
Still in Portugal, there's only so many museums	66
In the Spanish civil war, Orwell himself was shot	67
In the evening, we walk Porto a bit,	68
We take the Metro together to tour	69
The curator of the Palacio Marques de Fronteira	70

Morocco in June

The chaos of a large urban airport in Lisbon	73
Morocco. Travel-fatigued, I am dismayed by Casablanca	74
Morocco has begun replacing highway signs	75
Leather and weaving workshops line Chefchaouen's	76
On the road between cities—Fez, Meknes—we stop	77
Along the way, we learn many things from Lahcen	78
We meet our guide for the day, Mohammed,	79
We spend most of the day following Mohammed	80
Mohammed is one of ten children,	81
In Chefchaouen, Mohammed pauses	82
The intimate places in Morocco I'd not dare to enter,	83
Mohammed tells the story of three Chefchaouen	84
In the evening, we meet Lahcen in the village square	85

On the way to Fez, we stop at the Roman ruins	86
Then, it was on to Fez,	87
Waking in this Moroccan room of blue walls	88
At the Riad Ghita, we breakfast downstairs	89
We arrive at the Fez art cooperative Art D'Argile	90
We walk the Jewish Quarter	91
In Fez, we are ushered inside an immense	92
In the market, an old woman charms us	93
By mid-afternoon, we tell Rachad we are exhausted,	94
As we walk the streets of Fez, Rachad answers	95
We're on the road to Fattah's house,	96
Despite the delights of Morocco, Linda is a western	97
At another café with Rachad, I mine him	98
In the van, we ask Lahcen—our omnipresent driver—	99
Driving the endless highway, we angle	100
And then, the desert vanishes	101
Under the highway is a pedestrian tunnel	102
On the way to Fattah's house, Lahcen points	103
Fattah built his new home, Villa Ourti,	104
It is like waking inside a dream	105
I open Stephen Batchelor's *The Art of Solitude*,	106
Even in Morocco, I bring the world with me	107
Driving the endless desert in Morocco,	108
In the van, I move to the front seat	109
We wake to cold, gray skies at Fattah's,	110
Breakfast can take a long time at Fattah's,	111
As we drive to Marrakech, Linda leans over	112
On the road to Marrakesh, the goats balanced	113
Arriving in Marrakech is a revelation, a shock,	114
We discover that our guides—Mohammed, Rachad	115
A last evening in Marrakech—we wander the markets	116
The drive to Casablanca takes nearly three hours	117

Portugal & Spain, Again

After Morocco, the Lisbon airport in Portugal feels	121
This morning, Linda is up early exploring	122
Belém is a freguesia (civil parish) of Lisbon,	123
Along the sprawling riverfront of Belém,	124
We walk to an astonishing monastery in Belém,	125

In Portugal, as elsewhere, it's easy to romanticize	126
We spend an afternoon in the Jardim Botanico Tropical	127
Interlude: A Map of the Path So Far	128
Of course, then *we* arrive—famous personages,	130
Looking for our rental flat in Sevilla,	131
First full morning in Sevilla. I wake slowly	132
This small flat in Sevilla has two large double-windows	133
So, Seville, *Sevilla*...like a new date, I want to know	134
Roaming Seville, I find the *Archivo de Indies*	135
The bells of the Sevilla Cathedral ring out early	136
After so many days of travel, my brain and body	137
Here, in the midst of religious architecture	138
We walk round the corner from our flat	139
Finally, it is time to escape history—museums,	140
Two more days in Sevilla before we transit	141
The artist whose studio is adjacent the courtyard	142
We head cross-city through Sevilla's winding streets	143
The Seville weather edges toward 100 degrees,	144
Interlude: Portugal & Spain as Fraternal Twins	145
Waking slow in Sevilla.	148

Barcelona

The ninety-minute flight from Seville to Barcelona,	151
Barcelona has two artists woven inside its history:	152
From hillside views in Parc Güell one can see	153
Our second morning in Barcelona. We walk	154
Gaudí's Sagrada Família basilica exceeds my wilder hopes	155
Wandering old town Barcelona, we spy	156
In Barcelona, one cannot be true to the city	157

The French Countryside

The train from Nantes, France eventually brings us	161
Biking the French countryside, we are entranced	162
In the French countryside, I find little motivation to write	163
Our last day of biking the Loire Valley. We rise early	164

Italy in Summer

A long travel day brings us to Isabella's Flat	167
The heat wave in Europe is catching up with us,	168
Sitting in Isabella's Flat early morning, windows flung	169

I may stick with Turin because the Italian Torino	170
Isabella's apartment. I sit adjacent the floor-to-ceiling	171
In the early evening, Linda and I finally go out for a stroll.	172
This pilgrimage to old Andalusia leaves me with a bone	173
In the Turin evening, we leave the flat for a long walk	174
I find myself drawn again to the book in Isabella's flat	175
At Isabella's table again	176
At a café in Turin, I entertain the news for a moment,	177
I arrive at the Museo Nazionale del Risorgimento Italiano,	178
I wander the Gallerina Subalpina, an antique arcade	179
In Turin's heat, I laze in the cool of Isabella's flat,	180
Not wanting to dwell on a fire we can't control	181
Inside Turin's Mole Antonelliana is The Temple	182
The whole world feels afire. Yet I am desperate	183
As we wake in Turin, California goes to sleep.	184
In Turin, we wake to another day of the reality of fire	185
Far along the Turin bike path, we stop for a late lunch	186
The only way Heather, our caretaker in Shangri La,	187
In California again, I unwrap the old book	189

New England in Autumn

New York flooded the day after we left	193
On the bike trip through Vermont, our guide Alex	194
Biking through red maple trees in Quebec and Vermont,	195
Vermont is small. America is big.	196
Our biking guide Alex has another story.	197
At the tiny border-crossing between Vermont and	198
In the dim light of the Montreal museum,	199
We are driven to the Montreal airport	200
In Camden, Maine, sun streams through	201
In the corner Tibetan store, I watch visiting monks	202
Wandering Maine's small towns, I find Stone Soup Books	203
We pull into the dirt driveway of Cobb Hill CoHousing	204
We leave Cobb Hill CoHousing and breakfast	205
Kennebunkport, Maine in Autumn. Sunny morning,	206
Home again. Slept well in my own bed.	207
Acknowledgements	209
About the Author	211

Preface

AFTER YEARS OF WRITING POEMS in traditional lined or prose formats, I found myself experimenting—while traveling—with contemporary forms of Japanese *haibun*. The poetic form traditionally involves a journey, reflecting the seasons, and typically ends with a *haiku* giving some final flourish or perspective to the narrative. My own travels occurred over the course of several years intersticed between the pandemic, and the rise of climate change as a prominent feature of life on Earth.

I'd been preparing for this use of *haibun* for a decade without knowing it. I'd begun an [almost] daily contemplative journaling fashioned along traditional *zuihitsu* lines. *Zuihitsu*, or *Flowing Brush*, is a classical Japanese form derived from a Chinese literary tradition employing random thoughts, diary entries, reminiscence, poetry, and more. It emerged in the Heian Period (794-1185 AD), first seen in Sei Shonagon's *The Pillow Book*. More modestly, it became the loose framework of my journaling after beginning more serious [and humorous] Zen practice.

My wife and I began traveling again after the pandemic became somewhat endemic. I continued journaling and found that upon return, there were natural occurrences of *haibun* lurking in the narrative. Revisiting these moments, I would sit quietly till a *haiku* emerged. The freedom I feel in working with contemporary iterations of these forms reflect a cross-cultural literary inheritance that, like the Arabic *ghazal* or any number of inspired genres, transform any new reader and writer as much as they are transformed. Our globe is inescapably mycelial in this way, intermeshed beneath the ground of the written word.

Underlying this series of journeys—through the great Midwest of America, Portugal, Spain, Morocco, a bit of French countryside, Italy, then later through New England—is an experience of pilgrimage. As I wrote in my journal then:

> We intended this trip to be a pilgrimage—which for us meant undertaking a meditative journey of discovery—not only of landscapes foreign and familiar in the outer world, but interior worlds enlarged by the very act of travel.

The Japanese poet Basho is of course an inspiration for such adventure. His famous book *The Narrow Road to the Interior*, which chronicled travels across Japan, served to explore both "interiors": of countryside and heart-mind, both. The ancient Zen poets grounded their work in Nature itself, the passing seasons infiltrating words with blossom and decay. Now, climate change appears as the ubiquitous background in our own travels. For us, it included a cataclysmic fire back home that we watched unfold at the end of our sojourn in drought-stricken Turin, Italy.

Which is perhaps too much of a spoiler, but this story is included in the journey that follows. We begin with a wedding in the great Midwest, before my wife began a two-week solo walk along the iconic *Camino de Santiago* pilgrimage trail in coastal Portugal—and I, a cross-country train trek back to California before joining her at the end of her trail. And the beginning of the next legs of our astonishing and simple travels, through a world aflame with beauty and change.

A few notes on the text that follows. The Table of Contents lists part of the opening line of each *haibun*, since the narratives have no titles.

Haibun 俳文 as a literary form combines prose and *haiku*. The range of *haibun* is broad and frequently includes autobiography, diary, essay, prose poem, short story and travel journal. The *haibun* typically includes a *haiku* at its end. In this text, I often use quotes from news sources, books I am reading, Wikipedia entries, poem fragments, the occasional black-and-white photograph, and more. These illustrate the striking and intimate features of *haibun*. Connecting the dots of the wide world.

English language *haibun* has become a new poetry genre over the last 20 years, with regular print and online publication outlets. Both *haiku* and *haibun* evolved from traditional Japanese verse in much the same way that free verse poetry emerged from traditional metrical and rhyming Western poetry.

Haiku is a Japanese poetic form traditionally consisting of three lines, with five syllables in the first line, seven in the second, and five in the third. While most *haiku* still consist of three lines, today English language *haiku* rarely follows the 5-7-5 (17-syllable) format, which stemmed from a misunderstanding of Japanese sound units (which are shorter than English syllables). The average English language *haiku* is now just long enough to be said in one breath.

Variants also occur, in both the number of lines, and syllables:

One or two lines

The most common variation is one line, sometimes called a *monoku*. The one-line form is based on an analogy with the one-line vertical column in which Japanese *haiku* are often printed. Some experiment with extending a single line into two, to elicit breath-breaks. These variations create a variety of ambiguities allowing for multiple readings of the same *haiku*.

Four or more lines

Haiku of four lines (sometimes known as *haiqua*) or longer have been written.

One word

A single word may occasionally claim to be a *haiku*.

>   Dane Cervine
>   Santa Cruz, California

[Note: Unless otherwise indicated in the text, the *inset* quotes and asides in these *haibun* are paraphrased excerpts from internet content, or poem excerpts from authors noted in the narrative. The *italicized haiku* at the end of each *haibun* is my own, and forms a part of the formal *haibun* itself.]

The Midwest in Early Spring

Here from California for a Catholic wedding, I detour toward the Left Bank Coffeehouse in Covington, Kentucky, across the river from Cincinnati, Ohio. The sacramental coffee. The body of scones. I walk along tattered blocks and upscale restaurants alike, find myself at a Harry Potter-ambient store named *Hierophany & Hedge–Reagents, Wands, Talisman, Bespoke Arcana.* It sits several blocks from the towering Mother of God Church where the wedding will be held. Pagan and catholic in the same town, and not burning each other. This, a kind of hope.

A newspaper trumpets the arrival of the magic shop:

> *Owned and operated by the mononymous Coil and Augur – two intentionally mysterious and impeccably dressed shopkeepers who look to be plucked straight from Victorian aristocracy... Immaculate antique woodwork, jars of curious powders, gemlike stones glittering in the warm sunlight, a wall of handcrafted wands made from woods sourced across the world... Is this really in Kentucky, or are we in 19th-century London?*

Who would think to find pagan magic like this in the Midwest? With the Catholics a few blocks away, the body and blood of Christ its own magic—an incantation etched on brass plaque of the brick wall:

> *The Annunciation of the Ever Virgin Mary, Mother of God. Organized 1841 by Rev. Dr. Ferdinand Kuhr, Mother church of German parishes and second parish in Covington.*

Which brings me now to the brick patio of The Left Bank Coffeehouse where heresies abound. The sky is edging into blue, the birds are singing. The weather app said a rainstorm would herald thunder and lightning, but this psychic of the ethers has changed its mind again. Ah, prophecy. I finger the maple wand I bought, thirteen and 15/16 inches, carved in Canada. Point it at the Mother of God edifice, make a spell.

> *May this marriage make*
> *your blood*
> *sing*

AND WHAT A WEDDING IT WAS, at the Mother of God Catholic church—immense stained-glass windows, colorful paintings of the whole gang—Mother Mary of course, Jesus, saints, the heavenly hosts. The bride and groom dwarfed by immensities, yet nestled in the bosom of centuries. Church pews filled with family members from near and far. After the traditional Catholic Mass, family photos taken, we walk the short distance to a downtown auditorium for the reception. And, to view the running of the Kentucky Derby on the colossal screen. Red Strike, an 80-1 come-from-behind winner, stuns everyone for the biggest upset in Derby history. A good omen for the married couple!

But, oh my, the cacophony on the vast downstairs conference floor! Can barely hear anyone talk, and it just goes on and on. I take several short walks for air, till dinner finally comes. Linda and I muse, ruefully, that this is certainly the setting for a super-spreader event—but so is much of Covington on this Kentucky Derby night.

Still, it is a wedding of celebration, and most everyone is having a fine ole' time, come what may. Now, an *endemic* rather than a *pandemic*. The human species, like Red Strike, running against the odds into the jubilant night.

> *Bride and groom kiss*
> *The mothers swoon*
> *again*

BETWEEN COVINGTON, KENTUCKY, AND CINCINNATI, bridges span the great Ohio River. I love bridges. After the wedding, I wander over the John A. Roebling, return via the industrial Clay Wade Bailey to an historic Main Street. Enjoy a luscious spell at Piper's on the corner of W. 6th and Philadelphia in a lounge chair, sip a chocolate shake and coffee concoction served by young Kentuckians in white shirts with names sewn in red on their chests. A throwback worth the moment. I open a magazine folded in the back pocket of my jeans, find the essay WHY THE PAST 10 YEARS OF AMERICAN LIFE HAVE BEEN UNIQUELY STUPID with a picture of the Tower of Babel by Nicolás Ortega, a fine question for an aging California poet. The author Jonathon Haidt says of this biblical story,

The text does not say that God destroyed the tower, but in many popular renderings of the story he does, so let's hold that dramatic image in our minds: people wandering amid the ruins, unable to communicate, condemned to mutual incomprehension.

The story of Babel is the best metaphor I have found for what happened to America in the 2010s, and for the fractured country we now inhabit. Something went terribly wrong, very suddenly. We are disoriented, unable to speak the same language or recognize the same truth. We are cut off from one another and from the past.

Perhaps it's always been like this. The cacophony of dialects and paradigms, fractured alphabets spelling out enemies and privilege, the very thing, perhaps, to keep things interesting. A great river divides, and makes a bridge what it is. Well, deep thoughts like this peter-out when the chocolate and coffee are gone, so I rendezvous with family at the Cock & Bull pub with its raucous charm, debate the great issues of the day where a pint will make you feel uniquely stupid faster than anything.

> *The wide river dares*
> *the bridge*
> *to cross*

I'D WANDERED CHICAGO ALL DAY, avoiding the immense TRUMP hotel sign directly across from our tiny upper room window. Some histories are impossible to escape. Exhausted, I pause at the river with my Ghirardelli chocolate ice cream cone melting in hand, discover I am standing on The DuSable Bridge—named for the Founder of Chicago, *Jean-Baptiste Pointe DuSable*. I had no idea. The reason I love history, its many surprises. His handsome bust peers still at the river. The plaque reads:

Jean-Baptiste Pointe DuSable (1745-1818)

African-Caribbean, born in St. Marc, Haiti.

In the 1770's he opened the first trading post beside the Chicago River, establishing the settlement that became Chicago.

The DuSable homestead was located near this site.

No one knew his parentage or history. He married a Potawatomi woman named Kitihawa in native tradition, then later by Catholic ceremony in Cahokia, Illinois Country. An impressive man, yet nearly anonymous now as I am—a tourist among the forgetful hordes.

I wonder what Jean-Baptiste would have thought if he'd remembered his dream that night in the trading post, of a gleaming city right where he lay, buildings like heavenly towers, the sleepy river alive with commerce only a trader would think divine.

> *Last night the river*
> *dreamt it was*
> *loved*

LINDA'S LAST MORNING IN AMERICA, before her Santiago pilgrimage ending in Spain. I will return west by rail to California, before eventually joining her. As she putters in the hotel, we reflect on all we've seen here in Chicago.

Not just the exteriors of architecture and gardens, the helter-skelter of traffic and pedestrians—the interiors are just as evocative.

Art, a way of climbing inside a city, a century. The museum, a portal.

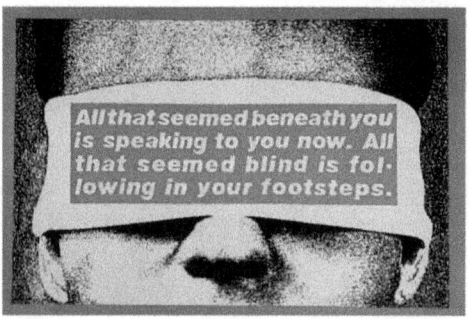

Standing in line for a ticket, the poster seems prophetic. The walls filled with omens, the battle for visibility, as in Leonora Carrington's *The Chad (O las hystericas)* which in old Welsh means *battle*, the subtitle *hysterics* a nod to the Spanish psychiatric hospital she was admitted to after the Nazis imprisoned her partner, the artist Max Ernst. And Dali's *Invention of the Monsters*, drawing on Freud and Breton, reflecting "his anxiety over a world without safe haven, a world indeed the invention of monsters." And finally, the bust of a young satyr—mythical creature half human, half horse—thrusting his hand out through the mouth of the immense theater mask he wears in a gesture both mischievous and menacing.

This *Silenos* became the chief comic character of Greek tragedies, when buried instinctual forces needed time on stage. Leaving Chicago, I am fortified by this art, carry its hysterics like a horse riding into battle against the monsters that rule.

> *Art is the everything*
> *that happens*

THE JOURNEY WEST FROM CHICAGO TO OAKLAND on the California Zephyr train begins. Already, it is full of mystery and revelation.

Someone calls out on the intercom "31, 31 Flowers." Train-speak. An aural oracle.

As we leave the station, I spy "The Purpose of Art..." graffiti on the side of an abandoned train car, the purpose itself obliterated by wear and tear.

Train passing the other way on the track adjacent ours, just feet away...so close we could touch or crash.

After leaving the suburbs of Chicago, with its gaggle of trainyards and backyards and small towns edged against the tracks, we hit a stretch of wide Illinois farmland as far as the eye can see.

Princeton, Illinois: the first (brief) stop. You can stare straight into the heart of the town from the small station platform. A pretty picture postcard of Main Street, America, if you will. Then, one small hamlet after another as we travel, each with a dream, a street, a chair to watch the passing show.

Over the intercom, they announce that rail-work had just finished ahead, and we'll be traveling at a sizzling 15 miles/hour for the next 7 miles. We're in Iowa now. It's difficult to know whether to be in a hurry or not.

Ottumwa, Iowa...our latest "fresh air" stop, to smoke for five minutes (its own oxymoron) or stretch legs. The name of the town itself, a pleasure. And for good measure, we get to see two immense water purification storage tanks, a handful of random small pine trees planted nearby.

The orange sun is setting behind a rich palette of horizon clouds. The plains receive the train like a tiny being only a mother would love.

> The extraordinary grace
> of wide open
> spaces
>
> in the heart
> of every
> thing

I RELISH THE SINGLE RED ROSE ON WHITE TABLECLOTH in the Amtrak dining car, the fine fare, as though I were more than an average American traveling west. As the Nebraska landscape rolls by, I read an essay in *Parabola* entitled "A Purpose to Be Served — Memories of P.L. Travers," subtitled "She wrote *Mary Poppins* and studied with Gurdjieff." What a tough-as-nails romantic old broad, elegant and whip-smart, such a woman of her day.

> The cauldron of plenty in each of us seethes with its ferment, sweet and bitter...the aching question of who we are and for what made, answered only by its echo; the need to stand before the Unknown and never ask to know; to take our leave of the world, head high, no matter how hard the parting...

An avid reader of Hinduism, Islam, she studied with a Zen master and led a Gurdjieff group in London for years.

> When we are born, she wrote, we enter into an obligation—"there are no rights of any kind, but only a purpose to be served." The hero (of whom every person is a type) is the one who "puts his foot upon a path not knowing what he may expect from life but in some way feeling in his bones that in some way that life expects something from him."

> ...you can only be the hero of your own story if you accept it completely."

Once, at the end of a talk about Fate in the old stories, a woman in the audience rebuked her: "I didn't ask to be born!"

Travers replied sharply: "I'm sure I did! I'm sure I insisted on it!"

Whatever the metaphysics, I decide to be more like Travers. Not knowing what I can expect from the journey, but in my bones, vowing to offer every last inch of this fathom-long body.

> *When I wake*
> *the Rockies loom like giant*
> *answered prayers*

MEANWHILE, CARRIED WEST IN MY TINY AMTRAK CELL, I turn to *The Banished Immortal – A Life of Li Bai*, by Ha Jin, for a glimpse into another traveler's life many centuries ago. He lamented his homelessness, yet chose to wander old China in search of a "higher order of existence."

> But for now, he was to roam...as a miraculous figure of sorts, as people later fondly nicknamed him the Banished Immortal. This moniker, which he embraced readily, implied that he belonged to heaven and was here only because he had misbehaved up there. It became essential to his sense of identity...

Watching the intimate landscapes of Indiana, Illinois, now the Far West drift pass the train window, Li Bai's notion of "the Banished Immortal" strikes me as romantic but partial—as though his world was but a dim reflection of another paradise. I can't fault him for this, the affront I felt at the inescapable Trump Hotel moniker in Chicago, the way we seem bent on ruining this given paradise. Still, watching the tiny towns of America's great plains meander by, I can't help but love the tattered lawn chairs and battered picnic tables edged toward the tracks. Empty, for the most part, though enough for hope: that someone is enjoying the great show, here. This all-too-mortal paradise.

> *The train whistles—*
> *the wide plains*
> *echo*

Linda and I both feel this grandparent-season of life like contrary magnets: stay close to home, but see the world before death comes. Our grown children now having children in the same town we bore them in—it's quite the allure. Though some travel far just to keep in touch. This earth axis, pulling us across revolving hemispheres by privilege or necessity. Criss-crossing continents for holidays, weddings, deaths. Or just to see—bear, moose, deer, certain trees or mountain snows—while we can. We, like birds or whales, even tectonic plates, migrate when pulled, magnetic, round this globe. Returning, when we can, to home.

> *The entire Earth*
> *is family*

TRAINS ARE GOOD FOR REVERIE. They can make a studious meditator out of the dullest of passengers. In the Amtrak view car, I spy sky and mountains simultaneously, interrupted by pages of this *Lapham's Quarterly* edition on "Migration." Spurring movement north from the southern hemisphere's growing heat waves, drought, surging populations, unimaginable evils. But the opening essay by Sonia Shah says this is an incomplete view—the unpredictability of cultures merging, and what emerges from this mix, is how the *new* comes into being. She says this as "the daughter of Indian immigrants" who bore her in New York, where she studied journalism, philosophy, and neuroscience at Oberlin College. She says,

> ...by the mid-twenty-first century, climate change will create an army of 200 million environmental refugees, who will scour the planet. Migration will be "one of the gravest effects of climate change"... could even lead to civilizational collapse...it has happened before...
>
> It's possible that our restless ancestors, rather than reluctantly escaping from bad conditions, capitalized on good ones. The earth's orbit wobbles on timescales of tens of thousands of years...from elliptical courses to circular ones... Such climate swings...facilitated human migration, by turning the impenetrable deserts of North Africa, for example, into habitable savanna-like green corridors across which humans might have moved, like butterflies and clouds of pollen across the forests along the Savannah River...
>
> Like butterflies and wolves, human migrants change the ecosystems they enter...

The birth-rates in much of the northern hemisphere are falling like flagging leaves. Fewer to carry on, work the shifting fields, become the next presidents, buoyant entrepreneurs, migrate to newly navigable artic seas. It is a privilege to welcome those who migrate. It might be our only hope.

> The shifting scenery
> itself is
> home

THE AMTRAK BREAKFAST REMAINS A MODEST but solid affair. I sit with a man named Michael who is accompanying his son from Chicago to Denver for concussion treatment. The son apparently has had seven over the years (he didn't specify if sports related), and stays in the train roomette under low-light conditions. Michael is an earnest Catholic business man with a love of history, and we share stories as though children of the same mother. As though the rise and fall of empire, each terrible war, the exhilarating eras of peace, exist now, here, in this speeding train. Along with his son, quiet in the dark, whom Michael doesn't speak of again. Instead, recounting the many bike trips taken over the years: Viet Nam, Croatia, South America, this northern hemisphere. The thrill of the journey. Though I imagine his son's: the topographic maps of brain- imaging, powerful magnets and radio waves revealing the invisible injuries of the human. And now, Denver—where his son will emerge from the dark, work his way as another child of Earth toward light too bright to bear.

> *The sound of railroad tracks—*
> *a metronome*
> *a pulse*

We've been ascending the eastern hills outside of Denver into the Rockies proper, seen from my perch in the View Car. Not bad. We'll pass through 43 tunnels, most of which are brief, though the trek through the Moffett Tunnel we're in now lasts nine minutes, the longest tunnel on the California Zephyr line. A seeming eternity underneath the earth. The rhythm of light then dark

then light lulls one as a mantra, or the fingering of prayer beads. A tunnel feels oddly familiar, like the birth canal that brought me here, or the final tunnel past arrival emptying into ultimate light or darkness. Or perhaps the journey is endless, just with a different view of things—like this train: not above from vast atmospheric realms, nor captive to the slow movement through cities. Rather, one sees the backside of terrain heretofore invisible—the tiny hamlets of the Midwest, intimate, with names like Silt, Antlers, Rifle, Parachute, and the ones too small even for a name. Just a single weathered house, a broken barn, someone singing in the garden.

> *In a tunnel, I'm never clear*
> *whether dark or light*
> *is my favorite*

OUR TRAIN ENTERS NORTHWESTERN COLORADO, near White River National Forest. The mountains are now red clay in color, with the variegated geologic patterns we fell in love with another time in Bryce Canyon and Zion. These immense layers of time.

Except—this is how it goes with trains—we end up dead-on-the-rails for 45 minutes in a deep canyon while repairmen work on a stretch damaged by rain run-off. To entertain us,

the train-announcer regales passengers with the story of the immense stone retaining wall we are stubbornly parked next to: how Swedish "second sons" came to America [since their elder brothers inherited everything], worked their way across the country as skilled masons. Here, though, it was too treacherous to haul cement given the steep terrain, so the stone wall we pass, piled high with large red rocks, were placed by hand without any mortar—and have survived intact till now. A good story. Just in time for the train to inch its way again through the narrow passage west.

> *Red clay valley stitched*
> *with rails—this*
> *enigmatic gate*

BREAKFAST IN THE AMTRAK DINING CAR. Utah, edging into Nevada—landscape of the prophetic. I read a *Parabola* issue entitled "Ancestors," Lipsey's essay "Prophets without Robes or Staffs: Hammarskjöld, Havel, Mandela, Thunberg." He profiles each as a "modern prophet" — I'm struck by their humility and resolve. Dag Hammarskjöld, the UN Secretary General from 1953-1961, helping shepherd the world past two devastating wars and aim toward sanity. The "ancestor" that guided him was Meister Eckhart (13th-14th centuries), his spirituality making the impossible quest for world peace possible. He addressed his God thus:

> *Long ago you gripped me... Now into your storm.*

Dag died in central Africa in 1961, plane shot down by unknown antagonists. Then, the poet-statesman Václav Havel, elected president of Czechoslovakia in 1989 after another prison term for dissent against the communist regime. He, too, was immersed in a spiritual awareness that fueled his social justice efforts—calling it *Being*. While in prison, he'd write obscure, convoluted letters to his wife Olga to bypass the prison warden's censorship—later published as *Letters to Olga*.

What strikes me about both men is their utter engagement in the "bowels of the beast" of this world, yet maintaining primary allegiance to a larger sense of *Being*. Their spirituality wide and generous enough to not demand fundamentalist adherence to a particular religion or politic. Nelson Mandela, better-known and revered, emerged from brutal imprisonment in South Africa after 27 years to "father a country," become ambassador to a world on the brink. But it is the young Greta who mesmerizes and annoys the current powers—a woman who knows she is a prophet, and that she shouldn't be:

> *This is all wrong. I shouldn't be standing here. I should be back in school on the other side of the ocean. Yet you all come to me for hope? How dare you! You have stolen my dreams and my childhood with your empty words. And yet I'm one of the lucky ones. People are suffering. People are dying. Entire eco-systems are collapsing. We are in the beginning of a mass extinction. And all you can talk about is money and fairytales of eternal economic growth. How dare you! ...*

But the young people are starting to understand your betrayal. The eyes of all future generations are upon you. And if you choose to fail us I say we will never forgive you... The world is waking up. And change is coming, whether you like it or not.

Nevada in late morning light looks like a land of prophets. The train barreling through gray-brown moonscape as though we already live on another planet. Where Greta has become the mother of us all.

In the desert, the light
is too bright to endure
for long

Well, the California Zephyr train drama continues! After more delays, fellow passengers with connecting flights or other business begin to panic. The train staff are marvelous, but didn't count on the length of these delays either, so there's no dinner, and the bathroom tanks are at capacity: you can't flush the toilets!

Terrence, the train's esteemed and gracious host manages to scrounge some beef stew for us, and it's pretty darn good. I do wonder about Amtrak and the larger railway system. They can't do business this way and *stay* in business—like America—so I'm curious how repairs and colliding freight-train schedules work. Hoping it's not the end of civilization as we know it—just normal business-model problems.

It's probably the end of civilization as we know it, is what I think as we pass through unidentified areas of northeastern Sacramento. An impressive array of homeless folks have settled in every nook and cranny of the industrial area that parallels the train tracks—or rather, they've fashioned their own homes and aren't necessarily homeless, so to speak. A spectrum of tents and tarps and trailers and old vans and more. Impressive and disarming at the same time. Terrence, for his part and ours, is grateful for the remaining beef stew he portions into each blue plastic bowl.

> *The rainbow tents flap*
> *like prayer flags*
> *in wind*

Portugal in May

SURREAL—I WAKE IN CALIFORNIA TEXTING LINDA IN PORTUGAL, at the end of her day walking the Camino pilgrimage trail. Yet the communication is nearly instantaneous. The ethereal waves circling our planet are real, it seems. Carrying messages, vibrating the web of things.

These last days at home before joining her in Europe is a discipline in itself. To be *here* till I'm not. I suspect I too am on pilgrimage, will turn 66 years of age there, somewhere, and if I hope for anything it's some inkling of a new turn on this road into my latter years. Or perhaps, simply a *return* that makes us feel enriched, but glad, in the end, to be *home*.

Which leads to my morning reading—Alan Watts' *Just So*, the section "Now Is When the World Begins."

> *Everybody is looking back over their shoulder and passing the buck—all the way back to Adam and Eve, and we know what happened there. They passed the buck to the serpent. And when God looked at the serpent, the serpent didn't say anything, because the serpent doesn't have a past—it's a wiggle. The serpent wiggles from its head all the way down to its tail.*
>
> *Are you a head or are you a tail? Do you move backward or forward? Which way are you going... It just wells up out of a mysterious present, always new. This very moment is the creation of the universe. Now.*

In this now, I leave my maps and schedules tucked into the vast digital spaces of my tiny black smart phone. Cheating, perhaps, but I do like not-knowing every inch of the journey. I suspect the serpent knew: the only way to break free from the prison of a straight line is to wiggle the unknown.

> *Heads or tail—the universe*
> *wants to know*
> *as much as me*

The trans-Atlantic flight from Denver to Frankfurt, Germany had its usual spectrum of monotony, coziness, sleep-deprivation torture, and things to be grateful for. The miracle of cruising over the vast sea nearly eight miles above sea level, for one. As though Lazarus, raised from the dead, complained about the rags he wore. Or, like me, had to file a lost baggage report at the Santiago airport, wait three days for my luggage.

At the Hotel Alda San Carlos, I find Linda already in our room with food from a local grocer. She's just finished her Camino pilgrimage, and is eager for more. A complete zombie, I walk the travel torpor off after a kiss. We stroll old Santiago with its stone churches, fountains, shops, cobblestone streets, immense courtyards—such beauty, many tourists in some stretches. Of which we are two. Which is the strangest of disguises. In the shop windows, I swear I almost see our robes giving us away.

> *Tourist, pilgrim, zombie—*
> *which is the true*
> *disguise?*

It is my first full day in Santiago, while Linda has been trekking the Camino for over two weeks. We walk to Catedral de Santiago de Compostela for a full Catholic mass (though we are informal Buddhists), the immense cathedral full of patrons, pilgrims, and tourists alike. In such moments, I am gullible as they come. Organ music swelling. Mesmerized by the swing of an impossibly gargantuan incense brazier back and forth through the center of the church, toggled by priests pulling thick festooned ropes as fragrant smoke spews the air like a pagan dragon. I'd believe most anything in this moment. That we are worth saving. That anything can still happen on this smoking thurible of a planet.

> *The sway of the brazier*
> *like a hypnotist's*
> *watch*

[Note: The *Botafumeiro* ("censer" in Galician) is one of the most famous and popular symbols of the Cathedral of Santiago de Compostela. It is a large *thurible* that hangs by means of a system of pulleys from the main dome of the Cathedral and swings toward the side naves. It takes eight men to move it, who are known as "tiraboleiros."]

Then, we find the Museum of Pilgrimage & Santiago, a five-story history that begins in the basement with photos of Tibetans in the wilds of the Himalayas, moving up the floors through indigenous and Islamic treks, finally the Camino itself. The museum captures this well:

> *Pilgrimage*
>
> *There are many dimensions to making a pilgrimage in both the real and the imaginary world. The pilgrim embarks on a ritual journey in search of purification, perfection or salvation. Pilgrim, way and shrine are all essential elements of this journey...it establishes a special relationship between the earthly and the holy, between the individual and the group, and because the pilgrim is transformed along the way... The term "pilgrimage" is also used allegorically to express the similarity between a journey to a holy place and human life itself.*

After, we tour the cobblestone alleys for tee-shirts, underwear and socks so I won't walk naked till my lost luggage arrives. Hundreds of Camino pilgrims arrive in the courtyard each day, from far-flung paths across Spain and France, or like me, skip the line and fly-in from the other side of the Earth. Pilgrims and tourists come in many disguises, can be difficult to tell apart. Like the young strapping trekkers who began as far east as possible, boomboxes blaring on their shoulders, stunned into silence by the end of the journey. Or me, humbled inside my unearned Camino tee, happy to begin.

> Basho says the journey itself
> is home; the path impossible
> to lose

[Note: The Camino de Santiago is sometimes viewed as a metaphor for the trail marked out in the sky by the Milky Way in its journey towards the ends of the Earth (*Finis Terrae*). It is the earthly manifestation of a route through the heavens. Ancient traditions regard Charlemagne as the true creator of the Camino. St James (Santiago) appeared to him in a dream, asked him to open a way to his tomb. Esoteric, initiatic and mystical values are often put forward in relation to the emergence of the Camino de Santiago with primeval earthly forces marking out its path and its end.]

After a night of murky dreams, we catch a tour bus to Finisterre, the End of the World in ancient Roman thought, the furthest point West beyond which nothing was known. The Mediterranean the center of their world, the Atlantic an edge one must not sail too far into. Invisible geographies lay beyond—in no need of discovery.

It is the end-point of the Camino pilgrimage, where our daughter finished her post-graduation trek a decade ago, the "zero-marker" stone the same one Linda wants to be photographed at as the intrepid mother following her footsteps. And so it is, on a handsome sun-drenched day with the gleaming sea looking much like California's coast. That other edge of land impossible to conceive: where the end of world becomes a circle, and a pilgrim might offer amends to ancestors and enemies alike. At home, finally, in the unknown.

In my dream:
edges, mist, hidden
hemispheres

On the three-hour bus ride from Santiago to Porto, I chat with a young French student on his way to a volunteer stint re-foresting a region in Portugal. "I'm not a revolutionary," he says, just wants to do his part greening the earth again. Europe his landscape more than any single country. Nearby, Linda chats with a woman from Berkeley, of all places, who'd also walked the Camino. Portugal, twin to the hills of Marin and San Mateo, the Santa Cruz and Oregon mountains. The earth itself wrapped in familiar bands of latitude and longitude round its body. We could be long-lost cousins, any of us. The revolution of hemispheres spinning light and dark like a top from a child's hand, peering hard to see when it begins to wobble, needs another go.

The dusk in Porto
feels like
home

WRITING IS MY WAY OF WALKING, I TELL LINDA as we lounge on the couch in our Porto flat, and she laughs. This European journey as much an *inward* trek as an outer one through foreign territory. I can wander as I will, under this spell of Portugal. Not just gawk at passing scenery, but *imbibe* the histories, poetry, and politics of this region of Earth and touch, if lucky, its soul. Already,

I sound like a tourist intent on sounding like a pilgrim. This paradoxical *koan* of travel. We're in Porto for two weeks, time enough to open the tiny terrace doors when it begins to rain, and not go anywhere special. The eager cathedrals can wait, as they've done for centuries.

> *Important and ecclesiastical—*
> *rain drenches*
> *the old stone*

WE ARE ON PILGRIMAGE TOGETHER, each in our own way. The desire to leave familiar shores, break-out of the pandemic bubble with its rigor of sheltering-in-place. To travel broadly before travelling itself becomes impossible, whether from age or new pandemic or war. The usual chaos that, like weather, can surprise. But how to get inside the eyes, the experience, of old and young alike for whom America is not the center of the universe? For some,

like the young French student on the bus, America is a mysterious sprawl, "so very big," so foreign as to be unknowable, even with relatives in New Jersey ("Wherever that may be," he says). But his life is here in Europe. And I fall under its spell sensing the lives of older Galicians and Portuguese, watching them slowly walk to and from church, banter over cappuccinos and wine at cafes, families talking loud and happily, or quietly with pathos, as absorbed in their own worlds as I am in mine. But theirs has nothing to do with America,

and I'm spun by this vertigo in an unusual way. Falling in love with other countries helps me fall in love again with my own. Like an old marriage, that young ache still pulsing.

> *The garçom offers me*
> *wine as though*
> *family*

I TRAVEL WITH MY BOOKS. Portugal floats in numinous layers of thought as much as masonry, relics, statues. On the coffee table I unstack my pile: *Don Quixote de la Mancha,* by Miguel de Cervantes (illustrations by Salvador Dali); Federico Garcia Lorca's *Selected Verse* in bilingual edition; *The Last Great Cause–The Intellectuals and the Spanish Civil War,* by Stanley Weintraub. But it's the vision from the final book's subtitle—*The Ornament of the World: How Muslims, Jews, and Christians Created a Culture of Tolerance in Medieval Spain,* by María Rosa Menocal —that has me. Dreams of paradise lost, or still shimmering ahead. Even America across the sea now looks like empire, a quixotic horse, another last great cause, a tarnished ornament.

> *A book, like a horse*
> *is a country*
> *of desire*

EVEN HISTORY MUSEUMS DON'T KNOW THEIR OWN STORIES. I gather my wits for a deep dive into beginnings, a rabbit-hole maze of dizzying proportion. Portugal's history begins eons before "recorded" history, but there are glimpses.

> *From Wikipedia: Portugal is the oldest continuously existing nation state on the Iberian Peninsula and one of the oldest in Europe, its territory having been continuously settled, invaded and fought over since prehistoric times.*
>
> *It was inhabited by pre-Celtic and Celtic peoples, visited by Phoenicians, Carthaginians and Ancient Greek traders, and was ruled by the Romans, followed by the invasions of the Suebi and Visigothic Germanic peoples.*

The Visigoths saw themselves as inheritors of the fallen Roman Empire, as one day someone will with America, no doubt. But who the first peoples were is lost to a time before history. When sky stretched forever, the ground was sacred, and no one had first claim.

> *Beneath the ground lie*
> *embers of the first*
> *fire*

As with my own family history, the further I go back, the tangled roots disappear underground. The liturgy of remembrance, of names becomes a kind of poetry. Here, on the Iberian peninsula, there have been many peoples: Marcomanni, Quadi, Hermunduri, Semnones, Lombards. And later, the Alamanni, the Bavarians, and two kingdoms in the Migration Period referred to as the Suebi–originally from the Elbe river in what is now Germany and the Czech Republic, before the nomadic Huns swept them west. Identity,

tangled underground in webs of DNA and lost culture. Names, a flower grown from eons of mulch. As with tribes native to the "Americas," most knew themselves as unique clans with differing language and customs. But they knew one thing: to sometimes marry outside the tribe. Knowing the genetics of clannishness led to death—that the foreign ways of "the other" was sacred, the secret to life.

> *The roots of me*
> *flower in your*
> *eyes*

Spain, just over the Pyrenees, a brash older brother—the *flamenco* rather than the somber *fado*—but all is love now after war, like siblings. But the forgotten daughter, so to speak,

is everywhere [in]visible—the Iberian peninsula ruled for two centuries by Muslim "hero/villains" like Abd al-Rahman, who swept-in after exile from home in Damascus (family slaughtered by a rival Muslim clan). He established a marvel of a kingdom in what is now southern Spain and Portugal, fostered inter-marriage and cultural-integration with Jews and Christians as a path to flourishing. Before this world also passed into legend.

I can picture al-Rahman as a new arrival, marshaling everything Arab to imprint the buildings themselves with flowered designs, geometric patterns, pointed arches, tiles, water spaces, and calligraphy. Visible still, everywhere—a secret in plain sight. The missing key I've been looking for in understanding this western-most tip of the Edge of the Old World.

> *Families always have*
> *a child with a*
> *secret*

LIGHT RAIN IN PORTO, SO WE ARE HAPPY TO FIND SHELTER in churches and museums. Across the square is a modest Catholic chapel Igreja do Carmo, connected to its "twin church" by a narrow "hidden house" sandwiched vertically between the stone edifices—serving as a secret home during times of danger or attack. It is all quite musty and forlorn—an underground catacomb leads upstairs through a cramped stairway past tiny bedrooms, a tapered dining room with Baroque furniture, a slim library, a humble kitchen. A way to survive religious purges, militias, political feuds. When your life was, literally, at risk. In the old days, they say.

*The stone edifice magnificently tiled
in blue & white—the red,
catacombed*

[Note: Azulejo tiles decorate both the inside and outsides of many buildings in Portugal, and it's not uncommon to see the entire facade of a house covered in them. These iconic blue and white tiles have become a hallmark of architecture and beauty across Portugal.]

After the forlorn churches, we walk to the art museum Museu Nacional Soares dos Reis. However, major portions of its permanent collection are closed in order to rotate exhibits. It's as difficult, I imagine, for a museum or a country as it is for me: to display all that we are at one time. But we do enjoy what remains open: old historical paintings in a room darkened to preserve them; and a spacious exhibit of modern artists in rooms of endless white walls. The dark and the light of things, it seems.

The new statuary hall, too, is a metaphor in itself: empty except for three figures. At one end of the long chamber, a sculpted youth titled *Exile*–at the other, two stoic military figures, pompous enough to forget.

Outside, the spacious grounds sport lawns browned by drought, walkways lined with broken fragments of ancient Roman fountains, masonry, torsos with absent arms, heads.

Porto seems a land, like me, of contradictions that require the patience of time to display. Old history kept darkened to preserve. Open spaces that calibrate new light. I stare at the youthful exile for a long spell. Feel the eyes of old generals behind.

Not one explanation
in English

THE RAIN BEGINS TO LIGHTLY FALL AS WE WANDER another of the Porto museum outdoor areas, ancient masonry stationed widely apart in uncut grasses. I am grateful for the English description in the brochure:

> Lapidary Collection
>
> On exhibition at the Museum's Garden are stone objects linked to the history of the city of Porto. Most of them from the demolition of buildings (convents or chapels), fountains and walls, which took place in the late 19th and early 20th centuries, as a result of the city's urban growth.
>
> This nucleus includes pieces from the North of Portugal in stone, examples of architectural, funerary, heraldic and epigraphic sculptures—such as portals, chapiters, coat of arms, funerary stele, sarcophagi, milestones and inscriptions, ranging from prehistory to the 19th century.

As a poet, I love the sounds in these words: portals, chapiters, sarcophagi. I may have to use these in a poem one day. Just to hear the vowels of history, the consonants lowered again into earth.

> *A word is a portal to*
> *the nucleus of*
> *memory*

We head into downtown Porto having fetched tickets for noon entry to the mysterious Livraria Lello bookstore, with the enchanting central red wooden staircase ushering patrons to the second floor. A region, a country, a people, are more than its tourist destinations, old architecture, even its food (though some might disagree about the latter). To know Portugal is to be voyeur of its books and beloved writers. There are as many statues of literary figures as there are of generals on horseback. Poets are loved as intimate friends. And Fernando Pessoa's *The Book of Disquiet* embodies some essential aspect of soul in this Andalusian landscape.

> *I crave time in all its duration, and I want to be myself unconditionally...*
>
> *Inch by inch I conquered the inner terrain I was born with. Bit by bit I reclaimed the swamp in which I'd languished. I gave birth to my definitive being, but I had to wrench myself out of me with forceps...*
>
> *Perhaps it's finally time for me to make this one effort: to take a good look at my life...*

The cover is evocative—reading a smattering of entries, I fall in love with Pessoa's utterly strange language of soul. The narrator's multiple selves, his insistence that the real life is inside, hidden from view. The book description, haunting in itself:

> This unique masterpiece – unique because there is nothing quite like it in western literature – purports to be the "factless autobiography" of an assistant book-keeper named Bernard Soares, written in notebooks and on odd scraps of paper... The Book of Disquiet was left in a trunk which might never have been opened. The gods must be thanked that it was.

I buy the book as any tourist might, place it in my day-pack along with travel-guides and maps for Porto. But secretly, Fernando paces inside me, scribbling notes, inch-by-inch giving birth to my definitive being.

> *The Porto clerk eyes*
> *my book,*
> *smiles*

We cross the Douro River on the Pte. do Infante bridge, with beautiful views of Porto and the surrounding region. Walk the opposite bank to a park where we sit, listen to a mournful guitar-rogue dressed like a hippie wild-man serenade the Friday crowd for a spell. It starts to sprinkle, so we walk back over the Luis-I bridge, home to our rented flat as though we belonged as much as the rain and sun.

It must be the Andalusian air, this sense of being at home in the world. Pessoa writes:

> *An income sufficient for food and drink, a roof over my head, and a little free time in which to dream and write, to sleep – what more can I ask of the Gods or expect from Destiny? ...*
>
> *I realize that there are islands to the South and great cosmopolitan attractions and...*
>
> *If I had the world in my hand, I'm quite sure I would trade it for a ticket to Rua dos Douradores [the street he lived on].*

I am grateful to be on the same great peninsula of Europe as Pessoa and Lorca and the endless river of aspiring Celts and Visigoths and Romans and Christians and Jews and Arabs that have dreamt mercilessly about this modest stretch of Mediterranean clime.

> *The guitar spills over*
> *the Douro like*
> *rain*

[Note: *Rua dos Douradores* is a real street, just four blocks long, not far from the center of Lisbon. Nondescript, narrow and ordinary, too cramped to offer a good look at the buildings; still Pessoa wouldn't trade it for the world.]

IN OUR PORTO FLAT, A SUDDEN RAINSTORM causes us to open both "French" doors (perhaps here they are Portuguese doors, or American doors?). We can't resist the humid warmth, the thunder. Over coffee and eggs, I take a break from the Andalusian Middle Ages for the insightful Weintraub book, *The Last Great Cause – The Intellectuals and the Spanish Civil War*. Find myself a voyeur of war and its political conceits, as much as poetic *witness*. The book itself a testament to the choices many writers, intellectuals, and activists wrestled with as the Spanish Civil War unfolded in-between the two Great Wars. The romance of revolution drawing an international cadre to the front lines—ill-prepared, few bullets, little food. The brute realities of war. Yet, one must do something...a poem, a bomb, a body given in metaphor or blood. The thunder outside wanes

as I close *The Last Great Cause*, scan the headlines where, just north of here, Ukraine is being brutalized by Russia, again. Perhaps there is no last great cause, only the next one. And in between, the greatest revolution of all: peace. A small flat. Empty coffee cup, the remnants of yolk on a blue plate.

> *The rain falls—*
> *boundless missiles of*
> *water*

EVERY DAY, WE WALK THE RUA DE SANTA CATARINA near our Porto flat, with its cafes and street musicians, local merchants and international outlets alike. This practice of being a global citizen, marinating in other cultures as guests in the ancient sense. Nurturing beauty, rather than the almond-sized amygdala, the reptilian brain still pulsating at the base of skull in each of us.

Porto is the picture—eerily so—of a daily life lived also in Kiev, Ukraine, and cities like Odessa before the invasion. Just north of here—not an Atlantic or Pacific ocean away. When few could really imagine that days later, their lives—working, raising children, sitting in cafes—would be shattered. It is surreal, though,

how Portugal flourishes now from tourism itself. To share culture more than war, life more than death, a café seat rather than a tank's. The French philosopher Blaise Pascal famously wrote:

> *All of humanity's problems stem from man's inability to sit quietly in a room alone...*

and I want to do my part. Most days in Porto, I walk the Rua de Santa Catarina practicing peace, return to our flat along the Capela das Almas where a small church façade is covered in the blue tile azulejo mosaics famous in the region. Blue the color of sky and rain and soul. Then sit quietly in a room and compose this poem.

> *A handful of euros, an empty cup—*
> *the garçom is happy*
> *enough*

Roaming Porto's riverwalk along the Douro River. The crowded tourist areas merge imperceptibly till we find ourselves suddenly alone under a towering bridge. Steep rocky streets narrow as alleys angle up the cliffs, and before we ascend, a stone guide meets us at the base. We peer at the plaque beneath the woman carrying a heavy load:

Who were the Carquejeiras (Gorse women) of Porto?

They were women who in the late 19th century transported 40 to 50 kilos of gorse from the Douro River to downtown and surroundings of the city, through the hard and cruel sidewalk of Corticeira. They did not have a voice, they were not respected in their human condition, they were not praised, evoked or caressed by the hard and important work they performed...

"They were not caressed..." is the phrase that stays with me.

Yet art bears witness, and the city itself, and I gently run my palm along her rough skirt, feel the strength of her legs. Known as "iron" women, poor, fighters, they daily carried immense bales larger than their own bodies, the wild gorse used to light ovens in bakeries, homes.

After the long climb back to our flat with my tiny day pack, I flip open a beer, read more about *gorse*. In Brazil it is known as *carqueja*, used also as a medicinal tea. It tastes quite bitter, they say, but is the best medicine for a hangover. Which is the way of this life, perhaps—the bitter a necessary tonic for beauty.

> *My legs—not nearly*
> *as strong as*
> *hers*

[Note from a Portuguese commentator: Those women who made the stones of this street their daily rosary, I don't know if they knew how to pray...but they didn't need to, because the life they carried on was a river of tears, it was a face of suffering, and it was always a desire to love more those children they'd given birth to...]

WE SPY A LIBRARY-MUSEUM—THE MUSEU DA CIDADE—with a unique exhibit. Long rows of rare books—old occult and "scientific" topics—interspersed with sound-recording devices from another age: wax cylinders, a phonautograph, magnetic tapes. The text reads:

> RADIOSTHESIA – *Capturing, conducting, comprehending Invisible Forces*
>
> *The words are neologisms derived from two terms: the Latin term,* radium, *"radiation," and the Greek term,* aesthesis, *"perception via the senses." In the past, the term* rabdomancia *was also used, formed by the Greek terms for "rod," and "divination."*

I suddenly feel right at home in the eternal new age that springs each century in another geography before it wanes. Like a vast underground conspiracy or mycelial network, surfacing here in Portugal where the brochure announces:

> *Books are trees, libraries are forests.... Books are force fields. When closed, they harbour secrets. Once open, they operate as resonant force fields... When, and if, we open them, we enter new worlds. We encounter enigmas —things that have remained hidden since time immemorial, that allow us to connect with hidden yet palpable dimensions of our daily existence.*

This wedding of written and aural traditions. We amble in dim light from one showcase to another, viewing "archaic and archetypal objects that accompany us transgenerationally and transculturally." Antenna, pendulum, lightning rod, dowsing rod, radio, echo chamber, book, magnetic recording. Listen for the sounds of water, the ethers, restless spirits. The exhibit giving "rare access to obscure and hidden areas of the Biblioteca Publica Municipal of Porto."

The cathedrals can wait. The history museums with their generals and wars. Here, on an obscure corner in Porto, I listen. Ear-drum reverberating with subtle waves. Spine a tuning fork for the invisible.

> *There is no curator—*
> *the door simply*
> *open*

This morning, I keep in the spirit of Andalusia by beginning with Pessoa:

> *Let's act like sphinxes however falsely, until we reach the point of no longer knowing who we are. For we are, in fact, false sphinxes, with no idea of what we are in reality. The only way to be in agreement with life is to disagree with ourselves. Absurdity is divine.*

On cue, the sun breaks through the Porto cloudscape just now, illuminating the wooden floor and white walls of our apartment as though I've had an epiphany. But of what? The sound of seagulls wafts through, reminding of Santa Cruz, California. The sphinx in me unsure what my life is across hemispheres. Here, the not-knowing seems stark. Like now: the rain starts again even as the solar orb stares like a sphinx, unblinking.

> *Know thyself—this*
> *absurd, divine*
> *secret*

WE'LL TRAVEL TO MOROCCO SOON, SO I SIT CURBSIDE at a Porto café, considering. Arab architecture wreathes the square like a flower. The Andalusian narrative in Menocal's book shifts from Cordoba, to Granada, then Toledo. Each a Spanish city influenced by the Arab; and each, in their heyday, a world of feudal lords and *taifas* (city-states). Before Europe was a word, or America a country, or I a gleam in my mother's ancestral eye. To be intimate with a land is to know something of its story.

> In the post-Roman period Toledo, this craggy citadel, fortified by the encircling Tagus River, became the heart of the first independent Visigothic kingdom. The Visigoths entered Iberia in the beginning of the sixth century as Arians, a condemned version of Christianity. Toledo itself became a religious center, still thriving as one of the prominent cities of al-Andalus when Islam invaded.
>
> When the caliphate disintegrated, after the turn of the eleventh century, the peninsula fell into cultural and political rivalry among taifas. Toledo emerged as one of the most luminous and powerful of those independent city-states.

I look up "Holy Toledo" on my smart-phone, but the American vernacular does not originate with this Spanish city. It refers to a gangster-haven between Chicago, Illinois and Cleveland, Ohio where the police agreed to ignore the various Mafia families if they didn't wreak havoc in return. It appears in contemporary song lyric and Urban Dictionary lingo as something "unbelievable, disturbing, or that blows your mind." I am only slightly disappointed, though, since Iberian *taifas* were akin to gangsters, in the way that much of history is ruled when not dominated by an imperial empire like Rome, the Ottomans, Genghis Khan (the list goes on and on). But the secret thread

in Menocal's book is not empire, nor religious mafia, nor entitled families. It is the common light that falls upon my book, just now, illuminating shadow, filling the emptiness of my cup.

> *Crescent, star, cross—*
> *idol or flower*

HOLY TOLEDO INDEED! In the ancient city, libraries became a haven for ancient books saved from the abyss of war and decimation of culture by victors. I like this.

> *In the long aftermath of 1085, Toledo became the radiant intellectual capital of Europe, a Christian city where Arabic remained a language of culture and learning. A city with vast libraries of Arabic books, libraries begun long before additions by Castilian Christian monarchs.*
>
> *It was by way of Toledo that the rest of Europe—Latin Christendom—finally had full access to the vast body of philosophical and scientific materials translated from Greek into Arabic in the Abbasid capital of Baghdad during the previous seven hundred years.*
>
> *That a Christian city rather than a Muslim one should have played this role may seem ironic. But how surprising can it have been to Christians who prayed at that church at the highest point in the city, under horseshoe arches that echo those of Cordoba's mosque, and where Latin and Arabic writing together adorn the walls? [Menocal – edited for brevity]*

The secret arts of book, stone, calligraphy. The making of friends rather than enemies. I feel like a spy reading classified documents recalibrating the world. A new millennium? Another dark age? Revelation can be uncertain. The burning bush on the hill an oracle, or a warning?

> *Three prophets walk into a bar—*
> *the world depends on each*
> *staying sober*

We've another Porto week in this now-familiar apartment, with only a handful of commitments (bike ride tomorrow) before the train to Lisbon for two nights, then the flight to Morocco. A glance at the news assures the world is still the world, so I turn instead to the inner landscapes of Fernando Pessoa. After all, Portugal and this broader region of old Andalusia will be known more by its interiors than its cobblestone alleys.

> *To cease, to be the ebb and flow of a vast sea, fluidly skirting real shores on a night in which one really sleeps! To cease to be unknown and external, a swaying of branches in distant rows of trees, a gentle falling of leaves, their sound noted more than their fall, the ocean spray of far-off fountains, and all the uncertainty of parks at night, lost in endless tangles, natural labyrinths of darkness!*
>
> *To cease to end at last, but surviving as something else: the page of a book, a tuft of disheveled hair, the quiver of the climbing vine next to a half-open window, the irrelevant footsteps in the gravel of the bend, the last smoke to rise from the village going to sleep, the wagoner's whip left on the early morning roadside...*
>
> *...the silence of the apartment touches infinity.*

The page quivers in my hand, Pessoa's smoke rising still nearly a century after. To be lost in endless tangles is what a pilgrim might aspire to, here; while the tourist in me fumbles with his next map, marking the path with fluorescent yellow pen to ensure I never lose my way.

> *Our small flat*
> *ablaze*
> *with Infinity*

IN MY JOURNAL, I SIT WITH PESSOA AT THE WINDOW of a small apartment (his? mine?) and tell him what I think. He indulges me—it's not often he has visitors—listens patiently. I say that he can write as he does in the early 1900's of Andalusia *because* the Arabs invaded a millennium before, mixing indigenous with Roman, old Celtic, Visigoth, Christian and Hebrew till his world became strange enough to write. More polyglot than clerics admit. Pessoa

stares out the window, listening to the rain, but bids me continue. I say we are all one pathos, but many distinct threads of lyric, alphabet, faces, temperaments that no empire can sequester. And does he know how lucky he is! Because *after*, when the Christian world began to swallow again all of Europe, figures such as Peter Abelard, Judah Halevi, Peter the Venerable and more, kept ancient Greek and Arabic alive, and through them, even more-ancient Hindu cadences, sciences, alphabets, mathematics—skirting inquisitions, imbedding knowledge rather than excising it. It's difficult to know if Pessoa is

feigning interest, or lets each word beat against his ear-drum like storm. I press forward with my thesis: that he can write as an existential soul adrift in an unknown universe *because* the absent divine became more nuanced than what fundamental "Peoples of the Book" wanted. He nods with the practiced apathy that writers of his generation cultivated, looks me in the eye with one eyebrow raised. *I had no idea*, he says, and goes back to staring out the window while loud birds begin to squawk.

> *I never wanted to be*
> *a writer he says*
> *winking*
>
> *Cryptic as code—*
> *the black ink*
> *confesses*

WOKE TO WARM PORTO SUN OFF THE BALCONY. Today we'll take our rented bikes along the river, but for now, a bit of Lorca:

From *Poem of the Saeta*

> *Along the side street come*
> *strange unicorns.*
> *From what field,*
> *what mythological grove?*
>
> *Close by*
> *they resemble astronomers,*
> *Fantastic Merlins...*
>
> *Dark-skinned Christ*
> *passes*
> *from lily of Judea*
> *to carnation of Spain.*
>
> *Look here he comes...*

Mysterious. Yet the Andalusian peninsula is permeated by this dark pathos, this clear light. A mirror, I know, for whoever is looking.

From *Mirror Suite*:

> *Christ,*
> *a mirror*
> *in each hand.*
> *He multiplies*
> *his shadow.*
> *He projects his heart*
> *through his black*
> *visions.*
> *I believe! ...*

I'm in a country, now, of old mystics and poets. In this way I feel at home. And the Christ I'd grown up with in stark evangelical country is, here, full of mirrors and shadows. I too can believe in *this*.

> *Andalusia—where*   *And the bike ride—*
> *window becomes*   *more beautiful than*
> *mirror*   *salvation*

OUR PORTO CLOISTER AT RUA D. JOÃO IV, 376, apartment #304 is a quiet and modest gift. The small balcony looks over red-tiled roofs, courtyards with stray gardens, hanging laundry. The intimacies of neighborhood a more enduring legacy than battles and insurrections.

I finish the astonishing *Ornament of the World—How Muslims, Jews, and Christians Created a Culture of Tolerance in Medieval Spain*, by Maria Rosa Menocal. With its afterword about 9/11 and the fundamentalism still rampant across the globe, the book calls us to remember this Andalusian age—a "memory palace," she says, for what may come again. An image of Islamic, Christian, and Jewish cultures at their best, in contradistinction to much of what makes the news these days. Just across the way,

fundamentalists of every ilk plot the end of the world. In Jerusalem, Washington DC, Moscow, Beijing—as though there were only one world worth having.

> *A book, a balcony—*
> *invisible*
> *revolution*

In this lost land of old Andalusia, I read an essay "The Babel Within" by Gavin Francis, reviewing two new books:

> Memory Speaks: On Losing and Reclaiming Language and Self, by Julie Sedivy.
>
> Alfabet/Alphabet: A Memoir of a First Language, by Sadiqa de Meijer.

Themes of hybrid language and culture, the spaces between strident tribalisms. Sedivy writes of her draw to multiple linguistics and identities, much as the Andalusian culture embodies.

> I'm drawn, like a moth flinging its body against a light bulb, to in-between spaces and intersections, to hyphenations, to situations in which there will always be two sides... This is, for me, where all the heat and light can be found.

Regarding the loss of language and culture rampant in "normal" immigration and genocides alike, Sedivy speaks of her own: the loss of her birth language in moving to Canada.

> It was as if the viola section in the orchestra had fallen silent—not carrying the melody, it had gone unnoticed, but its absence announced how much depth and texture it had supplied, how its rhythms had lent coherence to the music.
>
> [Becoming fluent again in my "milk" language] has deepened and calmed my sense of who I am, forging a peace treaty between the various fragmented parts of myself. And it has cast a new light on the old question of how to make a home in a place that is foreign to your ancestors.

The other author, Sadiqa de Meijer, ends with an image of a fruit tree in the garden of a family friend unusually skilled at the grafting of branches:

> In his vegetable garden stood the odd, Edenic sight of an apple tree that also bore apricots and plums. Perhaps the minds of linguistic migrants are like that tree; the mother tongue is the apple trunk, with roots that penetrate the earth. And our later languages are branches, feeding through the same roots but setting their own fruit.

Traveling—becoming even a temporary migrant—arouses deep love for what is lost and found. Inside my own DNA are filial branchings of foreign vowels, shades of skin, embedded ancestors living happily in the trees of Africa—till a change of weather, the trees disappearing, the wide savanna beckoning.

> *This tongue-shaping*
> *new vowels like*
> *lovers*

Cloudy Porto skies. The haziness of sleep. This body of perception occluded by budding ear problems, wrenched back, time-zone warps. Still, in the morning I am happy to be sleeping next to Linda in this other hemisphere of the world. Waking, now, to make coffee and read Federico Lorca in his Andalusian landscape.

In our eyes the roads
are endless.
Two are crossroads of
the shadow...
from the road that starts in the iris
Adam & Eve.

The serpent cracked
the mirror
in a thousand pieces,
& the apple was his rock.

This original couple may have lounged as we do now. Before the land shattered, mirroring a thousand tongues-to-come, and endless ways home. I hope they loved moving into unknown territory. Even before Lorca, and the coffee that would come later.

The apple of knowing–
to eat or
throw

STILL IN PORTUGAL, THERE'S ONLY SO MANY MUSEUMS to gawk at, cathedrals to pray in or criticize. The fine food is endless, but you get fat, quickly. So I read *The Last Great Cause* about the Spanish civil war most Americans have forgotten. Big causes against big threats, competing utopias spawning apocalypse.

George Orwell was one of many idealistic writers wanting to "do something" to stem the tide of Fascism threatening Spain, and by proxy, the rest of the world. Arriving at the front lines of the revolution, it seemed a bad surreal film-spoof. Orwell saw action, but his commander said, "This is not a war. It is a comic opera with an occasional death." The young boys had few working rifles, most were museum artifacts that often backfired; little food, fewer boots or bullets, most of the time spent shivering in mud and fighting boredom. True to the old joke about the Anarchist's Code, another writer summarized the scene:

Para. 1. There shall be no order at all.

Para. 2. No one shall be obliged to comply with the preceding paragraph.

But what would I do if a general, or red-haired bully, tried to take over America? If I was not just on vacation, reading this old book—as though the threat existed only in fiction?

Apocalypse: utopia
at the end of
a gun

IN THE SPANISH CIVIL WAR, ORWELL HIMSELF WAS SHOT in the throat, survived eight days transported haphazardly to a hospital in Barcelona, escaping capture to finally arrive home in England. Disillusioned— that any political party or social revolution was "the answer"—all war devolving into chaos. Yet he still felt we often become our best selves in crisis. George suspected a greater war was to come after the Spanish conflict—a second world war. It became the fodder for his famous novels: *1984*, and *Animal Farm*.

> *If nothing else, the nightmare in Barcelona and the Aragon helped form such 1984 concepts as Newspeak, Doublethink, Thoughtcrime, and the rectification of newspapers in the "Ministry of Truth." For the adjective Orwellian we owe ironic homage to Catalonia.*

A writer may need every bad thing to make a good book. Like a soldier, enough luck to come home again. Put your feet up, disentangle the mind from thoughtcrime, doublespeak—say *truth* as though it was indeed a ministry.

> *Book pages flutter*
> *at the mention of*
> *truth*

In the evening, we walk Porto a bit, end up at a small family restaurant, O Buraco, and it is perfect. Seated in the back at a small table, we order salmon and sea bass, cooked as only the Portuguese do. No English is spoken, just eyes and hands and gestures. No one seems to hate us, nor privilege us in any way. As though we were *família*–that it was enough to be a human being. The sacrament of food, more precious than passport or blood.

> *The tongue needs*
> *nothing*
> *translated*

WE TAKE THE METRO TOGETHER TO TOUR the Palacio Marques de Fronteira, the multi-generational home of Portuguese nobles.

The palace was built in 1671 as a hunting pavilion to Dom João de Mascarenhas, 1st Marquis of Fronteira, who received his title from King Afonso VI of Portugal for his loyalty in the Portuguese Restoration War.

Seems there's always a war, and it's good to have friends. And loyalty. Descendants still live here centuries later, relying, though, on the paying public to keep their inheritance afloat. The "palace" reminds me of the Downton Abbey dilemma: how to keep legacy and grounds alive in the modern age. The gorgeous old stone residence with classic gardens is falling into beautiful ruin. Blue tiles, red and ochre walls, classic statues of Roman gods and frescoes to artistic divinities. Including, belatedly, the addition of *Poetry* since the Marquis loved it. The sculpture stares at me now—eyes quizzical, humorous. Knowing I will age much quicker than she will.

Green algae covers
royal pools glittering
with decay

THE CURATOR OF THE PALACIO MARQUES DE FRONTEIRA leads us from room to room in the old residence as though on a treasure hunt. Bids us examine the walls in one of the halls, look for hidden irreverences in the murals—like the *Where's Waldo?* books of childhood. Sure enough, amid religious iconography and pious scenes is a couple fucking in the bushes, a boy with a grin taking a dump behind the church, bare-breasted women toying with admirers. The old artisans had a sense of humor, and the family too. Almost daring visiting priests to notice.

Outside, too—pagan figures in various states of mischief adorn the chapel required of every Catholic household-of-standing. This minor rebellion to the requirements of state. Mother Mary keeping company with Pan, Jesus ignoring the mischievous satyr lurking around the corner, winking. In fact,

the curator says this delightful mix of Christian and Arabic, religious and pagan themes is a hallmark of this lost Andalucian world. Well, at least if you're a friend of the king. Manage to avoid inquisition when the powers that be shift, decide life is no laughing matter.

> *Blue murals—evidence*
> *in plain sight*

Morocco in June

THE CHAOS OF A LARGE URBAN AIRPORT IN LISBON—not knowing the language or the layout. Yet, as travelers do, we bumble and point our way through boarding passes, security, passport check-points. Strike up a conversation in one of the long lines with an American family from San Francisco traveling home with two pre-teen girls in ornery moods. As though this exotic world could not compete with the allure of their tiny phones. We wish them safe travels, take our short flight across the Mediterranean to Morocco, another world indeed. Our driver, Lahcen, holds a card up with Linda's name on it. Such a lovely, down-to-earth soul. Welcoming us as though we've finally come home.

The girls roll their eyes
in practiced
disdain

MOROCCO. TRAVEL-FATIGUED, I AM DISMAYED BY CASABLANCA and its airport environs. Old 1950's apartment complexes and urban sprawl. The coast littered with fenced-in motels or restaurants along every inch of sea. No Humphrey Bogart or Ingrid Bergman in sight. Lahcen, our grizzled-yet-gracious driver, says not to bother with the city unless you must. The interior is where it is beautiful. Still, we brace for a five-hour drive through empty desert that could be Nevada, or the moon. Windstorms stirring dust. The sky muddy and overcast, as though a postmodern artist had forgotten his color palette.

But after a couple hours, we wind our way into rugged hills toward Chefchaouen and the Rif mountains. The ascending scenery akin now to the hills of Mariposa, or Sonoma, or the modest mountains of El Portal before they become Yosemite. Instead of a great valley, there is this blue city on a hill, painted fresh every year to attract visitors. The blue iridescent, provocative, alluring—as though the Seven Skies had become earth.

The dusty van
a caravan to
Jannah

[*The Seven Skies*: Muslims believe in the existence of seven skies or heavens. The seven skies, or *Jannahs*, serve as a reminder of the vastness and complexity of the universe, and the power and majesty of Allah.]

[*Jannah* is a girl's name of Arabic, Hebrew, and Latin origins. In Arabic, Janna means "gardens, paradise." In Hebrew, Jannah means "God is gracious," while in Latin, it is a variant of Janus, the god of beginnings, transitions, and doorways.]

Morocco has begun replacing highway signs to include the languages still essential to its peoples: Arabic, Berber, and either French or Spanish depending on the old colonial regions. As though a poet and translator were in charge. The various scripts are beautiful, especially for road signs. Chefchaouen in Arabic is, شفشاون in Berber: ⴰⵛⵛⴰⵡⵏ or Romanized as *Ashawen*.

Now, the original Berbers and the invading Arabs and the colonial Romans along with the French and Spanish, are like many places around the globe: a tapestry of such pathos it is nearly impossible to separate the threads without ruining the weave. Though everyone here is Muslim now, unless you're just passing through. The police keep tabs with our guide each day, almost invisible to us. It's a tough business. Each new wave reminding how easily the old erodes, the future shimmers or threatens.

> *The young flock to the cities*
> *return with a cell phone,*
> *straightened teeth*

LEATHER AND WEAVING WORKSHOPS LINE CHEFCHAOUEN'S steep cobbled lanes, as they have for centuries. In the shady main square of Place Outa el Hammam is the red-walled Kasbah, a 15th-century fortress and dungeon. The octagonal minaret of the Great Mosque rises nearby, still calling to prayer. The Ethnographic Museum keeps stories alive—Berber and Roman, Ottoman and Arab. There is no land not touched by many. But the people carry on as they always have: sewing, blacksmithing, carpentry, needlework, leather tanning. The young travel hours to shop in a mall, bring back clothes and gadgets to seduce or frighten parents. Everyone agrees the surrounding fields of cannabis are a good idea. Commerce, the great peacemaker. The mosques, though, are not for westerners. Some places are best kept sacred, or at least secret.

When the great call comes
I too lift eyes
to the minaret

though none can invite
me in

On the road between cities—Fez, Meknes—we stop twice to stretch, use the traditional "squat and go" toilets, find food. The first is a Western-style gas station with an array of meat and vegetable wraps. The second is one of the ubiquitous coffee houses lining the roads, where old men and young sit, talk, stare into the desert. An elder and his twenty-something son serve me coffee with a flourish and a warm smile. But they won't look at my wife—she is almost invisible, and there are no other women in the outdoor shop. I see the fire in her eyes, bring her tea to a table at the far edge. Where an old world ends, and another begins.

> *Old men sit and stare*
> *at nothing*
> *I can see*

Along the way, we learn many things from Lahcen about Morocco as he drives, though he is quite comfortable with silence, too. I want to remember all I can:

> The landscape is filled with small family farms, diverse regions growing a wide range of crops: wheat, corn, olives, avocados, apricots, bananas, watermelon. There are larger agri-farms near the big cities, but Morocco is still a land of small farms.
>
> Every village and town has its own mosque, though Lahcen says that few go, except during Ramadan—like Christmas and Easter Christians back home. The mosques are governed by the Ministry of Culture, though rich citizens will often build one then donate it to the government. Lahcen says that, really, hospitals and schools are needed now more than mosques. Seems free enough to say this, at least in the van.
>
> Here, church and state are one—the dream of most fundamentalist Christians in America.
>
> There are elementary schools in many towns that we pass: brightly colored, multi-hued, education that is free to children. We pass laughing kids everywhere, happy in their play. Colleges are available to some in the larger cities.
>
> The police are adept at hiding radar trackers unseen along roads—you're fine if you don't go over the limit, but if you do, they'll pull you over down the road by radioing ahead—you either pay 150 dirhams on the spot, or go through a later court date and pay twice as much. Lahcen drives very conservatively, and well.

At dinner, Lahcen describes the modern Moroccan world as having forever been changed by the omnipresent smart phone. Even little kids have them, mothers in full traditional attire chatter away while they walk the street, men on motorbikes or oxen-carts on the way to market. He loves his, pulls it out to show us. Traditional life, he says, may fade or simply take new shape. Even Allah, it seems, must embrace change or be relegated to a museum.

> *I have rarely seen a man*
> *so at home in his world*
> *as Lahcen*

We meet our guide for the day, Mohammed, in the hotel lobby. He is full of smiles and stories: tells us he is 37 years of age, grew up here in Chefchaouen, left to get a university degree in Morocco, and for a while, work in a factory before deciding to return to his hometown and become one of two dozen tourist guides. He knows each alleyway, artisan stall, secret Sufi enclave, like the palm of his hand. Is proud to show off not only *his* Chefchaouen, but the broader history of Morocco. Oh to be as in love with one's country as Mohammed is! Not so much the empire of it all, but the corner bakery, the blue walls, the stream where women still launder clothes despite the lonely washing machines silent in their alcoves. They'd rather chatter and sing together, Mohammed says, and asks Linda if she'd like to try her hand at scrubbing a rug in the traditional way. The women laugh as she kneels, throws herself into the fray, for a moment becoming them. One human being learning another.

> *The soap is lathered into froth*
> *like the sea*

WE SPEND MOST OF THE DAY FOLLOWING MOHAMMED through the "rabbit-warren" of old, beautiful streets, ascending and descending stone stairways along the spring-fed stream emanating from the mountain. Along the way are innumerable small cafes, just two or three outdoor tables, often empty, waiting; in stone alcoves vendors sell brightly colored straw hats. The hats are a staple of the town's history, traditionally worn by young women at festivals to let others know they are available; married woman wear similar hats but with a thick dark weave of strings showing they are already tied by marriage. Though now, everyone wears them indiscriminately. Mohammed says the young don't want to be bound, want to show their colors, shop for a boyfriend. Perhaps one day get a job in a city, become famous.

This small village—where
a tourist is famous for
an hour

MOHAMMED IS ONE OF TEN CHILDREN, with three married sisters, one in Turkey pursuing her education (not married), several brothers in town living in the family compound, two other children who passed away. He shares a sweet, humorous glimpse of his own attempts to date: the young Moroccan woman more interested in texting than the long letters Mohammed would spice with the Arabic calligraphy he studied in college. The younger generation, he says hopelessly, is only interested in Western capitalism. He is a man between eras: in love with the old ways, yet drawn to the modern. Maybe one day, he muses, a wife will appear, and children, and the family compound will still sing. For now, he heads down another blue alley,

stops in front of a modest door with a green plaque identifying the house as a *zaouis*, a turret-less mosque for Sufis interested in long daily practice, separate from the life of the community. This *zaouis* was built in 1903 by the followers of Shaykh Ahmed Ben Ajiba, who died in 1809. Mohammed prefers the communal, says his own father was an Imam, as his father was—not in the Sufi tradition, but a leader of daily prayers in the village mosque. I tell Mohammed he might be an Imam of this space *between* eras. Sharing Morocco with strangers who'd otherwise be on the outside of its life. Here, in these blue alleys, where my wife and I hang on Mohammed's every word.

> *In the marketplace,*
> *the young women demure,*
> *the old women utter scandalous*
> *jokes*

IN CHEFCHAOUEN, MOHAMMED PAUSES in front of yet another blue door lining the curving streets like exits from a labyrinth. Each, a portal to a world I will never know. The doors are decorated with symmetrical patterns of black nails or bolts that, in the old days, documented family births through the generations. Doors that held many generations, doors "older than America as a country" Mohammed says. Suddenly, I feel blue vertigo as centuries whirl down the alley like wind. Though nowadays, the designs are mainly decorative, he says: families grow and move to other villages, to Casablanca, or across the Mediterranean. Lives like wind. Not a bolt. Not a nail in an old door.

> *The markets are full of eyes*
> *looking no further than*
> *here*

THE INTIMATE PLACES IN MOROCCO I'D NOT DARE TO ENTER, except with Mohammed. A small corner bakery where women bring dough they've made at home, have the baker insert in a low stone oven while they wait. They are in no hurry. It is quite hot inside, yet the women dressed in *hijabs* and layers of robe look nonplussed, even with small beads of sweat on the brow. They look at Mohammed and smile, continue their banter knowing we won't understand a word, and he won't reveal their public secrets. In the cold winters, he says the bakery is a warm haven from bitter cold. The young attendant is all smiles as Mohammed bids him hand me the ten-foot-long wooden spatula to place one of the loaves in the oven. He suspects I come from a world of such wonder, and I suspect the same of him.

> *The oven holds fire*
> *birthed 93 million miles*
> *away*

MOHAMMED TELLS THE STORY OF THREE CHEFCHAOUEN pilots and the failed revolutionary who languished in the king's dungeon after. Who somehow secreted a message through a sympathetic guard to his wife—a journalist in America—who managed to get FDR (Mohammed thinks that's the right president) to influence the king, as well as other European journalists, to finally release the jailed revolutionary. Mohammed proudly shows us a photograph of the now-older man alongside Mohammed—something he keeps close to his heart. He's not sure why. Something about different hemispheres of the globe touching. This impossible world where strangers can meet, become more than we were.

The photograph—
an enigmatic
promise

In the evening, we meet Lahcen in the village square as three handsome Gnawa tribesmen in traditional red and yellow robes play music, dance in hats with golden tassels. Famous for their music, the Gnawa were brought to Morocco as slaves from West Africa. After the abolition of slavery, they became a part of the Sufi order in the Maghreb region of northern Africa. Sufis are tricky, I know, and it's always difficult to tell who they are dancing for. A lost Beloved, perhaps Allah, a few coins, a country they once knew? Certainly not me, though they never look away. Eyes melting into eyes, dancing for the stranger who could be God in tourist disguise.

> *Lahcen, a Berber, hums this*
> *former slave song—in case*
> *Allah is listening*

On the way to Fez, we stop at the Roman ruins of Volubilis. The drive itself reminds me again of home: miles of terrain reminiscent of Los Banos or Mariposa, including roadside stands of fruit and vegetables. Though in Morocco, it's individual families bringing their harvest from the mountains rather than the agri-business outlets in California—and mosques, rather than churches. Latitude makes diverse regions of the earth similar in their differences. But we have nothing

like Volubilis in California. A full-fledged imperial outpost of Rome in its day. The empire came for the famous olive orchards, apparently. And well, because they could. It was hot as hell, but the video re-creates boutiques and baths, apartments and temples, that would have made it a paradise, for a while. Till the water ran dry. It was 100-degrees and we felt it, though Lahcen says it will get much hotter this summer. I move from shade to shade under towering stone pillars, imagine this empire of pleasure. How the centuries do what armies cannot: sweep hubris away like dust.

> *Earth, too—*
> *an empire of*
> *change*

THEN, IT WAS ON TO FEZ, one of Morocco's major religious centers. We arrive at the Riad Ghita, an astonishing multi-story home built in the 15th century which, like many homes here, shows its beauty only on the inside. The anonymous street corner is one of many, buildings with clay walls that stretch into neighborhood mazes. But inside, we find a towering inner courtyard of gorgeous tile surrounded by rooms with wooden shutters for privacy, or opened to the communal. We dine in this courtyard on elaborate pillows and are served one of the best meals we've ever had—a chicken tagine cooked on coals in the traditional way. Then climb steep wooden stairs to the roof to watch the night-sky rumble with lightning and thunder. As though Allah is welcoming us with danger and light.

> *Each door–*
> *a portal between*
> *worlds*

WAKING IN THIS MOROCCAN ROOM OF BLUE WALLS, geometric ceiling designs painted redolent reds and greens, blues and gold, elaborate stone white mosaic carvings arching over stained glass windows fitted with wooden shutters—it's like waking inside a Tarot card.

> *To live this way–*
> *beauty*
> *inescapable*

AT THE RIAD GHITA, WE BREAKFAST DOWNSTAIRS in the beguiling courtyard—spiced eggs, breads with the famous Moroccan honey, coffee, lime yogurt, chilled orange juice. We meet our guide for the day: Rachad. He, as with Mohammed in Chefchaouen, grew up in Fez and knows it like his own family. His mother and wife are Berbers, his father Arab, and he shares with us nuances of language and ethnicity that make Fez spring to life.

We drive through the imperial grounds with its seven immense gates, large restoration projects. Apparently there are thousands of families who have worked as servants within the grounds for generations, everything provided in return for their service. They rarely, and only with suspicion, leave the sprawling palace-fort complex. Some years ago, each was given a choice to leave and live on their own in surrounding communities, but most chose to stay—an exchange of unknown freedoms, Rachad says, for security, purpose, and tradition. University educated, he seems to feel it in his bones: this paradox of Morocco. What there is to find—or lose—in this changing world.

Each family—a palace
a prison, a way out
or in

We arrive at the Fez art cooperative Art D'Argile for a tour. As with artisan projects we've seen in Bali and Dharmshala, this one works to keep traditional cultural skills alive; here, it is ceramic and tile work. We linger for a spell as Linda works one of the clay pottery wheels after a demonstration by a quiet young man. He's worked this craft for many years, effortlessly creates perfect symmetrical vases, cups, bowls. Some artisans begin when children or teens, to "keep them off the streets," as well as preserve Moroccan culture. Blink, and they appear captive to this way of life; blink again, and I see them instead working fast food joints the world round, flipping a burger rather than clay, adding ketchup in tiny plastic cups rather than iridescent strokes of color.

The koan of tourism—
wet clay spinning
a world

WE WALK THE JEWISH QUARTER in the poorer neighborhoods of old Fez, though no Jews live here now. Rachad says there are perhaps a hundred Jewish families in all of Fez—most have left for Israel or Europe, though some still live in Casablanca. He leads us down tiny, narrow alleyways darkened by shade, shielding this immense world-within from the blazing sun. "Don't be fooled" he says—behind even the most beaten door lie large homes several stories high. The dark is glorious. Who lives here?

The adjacent market offers a clue—twist of winding alleys and throughways sectioned for particular craftspeople and wares: metalworkers, knife-sharpeners, brass bowl repairers, seamstresses, couch-makers, and of course food markets filled not only with every kind of vegetable, grain, fruit, but also a variety of fresh fish, snails, butchered cows of course, and even, grotesquely, a stall for camel meat, with a camel head hung from a hook, dripping blood from its nose.

But the lost community of Jews live mainly now as ghosts in an old synagogue preserved as a museum. We pay a small token to enter, and I am grateful since the mosques are not open to unbelievers. A Torah wrapped in burgundy-velvet with gold Hebrew calligraphy sits stoically in a dark wooden cabinet. We sit in silence on a hard bench, listen to Yahweh and Allah tell their story in different tongues.

> *Even the camel has a*
> *story*

IN FEZ, WE ARE USHERED INSIDE AN IMMENSE leather-tanning warehouse—traverse the retail areas open to tourist and local alike. The smells are overwhelming, but each visitor is given a sprig of mint to hold close to the nose. Each section is claustrophobically-filled with leather goods of all kinds in crowded wooden rooms. The jackets are alluring, but I can't bear the thought of trying them on in the stifling heat. Finally, the stairs ascend till we come to a balcony overlooking a stark "medieval scene," as the tannery guide says, because it has been in operation for a millennium. Long rows

of tanning vats of varying color sprawl vast as a football field, where hides are brought after meat is taken to the market. Each skin is dyed for weeks before made into leather sheets, which are then worked into belts, decorative bags, the ubiquitous jackets, even skirts. The rugged gentleman who leads this tour has skin leathered by sun that beat down on him when working the vats as a boy. *Very, very difficult work*, he says—but now enjoys providing tours, meeting people like us. It is nearly impossible not to buy something from him—men and boys laboring for centuries to eke a living from hide. But no matter how many jackets I try on in the sweltering heat, none fit well. It is stifling. It is hot. I finally wilt, buy some small trinket, a decorated piece of skin, a tattooed image burned in charcoal black, to remember.

> *A boy looks up*
> *at the balcony,*
> *stirring*

IN THE MARKET, AN OLD WOMAN CHARMS US toward her stall as she kneads dough into a thin sheet, places it atop a large, oval-shaped black "egg-head" to fry. Who knows how long she's worked this tiny shop? Her dark eyes beyond any stereotype reveal the young woman she once was, and now, the grandmother who looks directly into our eyes as though we, too, were her brood. The crepe-like *beghrir* is tinged with honey the color of each iris, and is delicious. We navigate

the thicket of tangled alleys under a roof of rugs and fabric, the shade saving everyone's lives. Mules angle the streets ignoring motor-scooters, both carrying a town one burden at a time. Rachad, our guide in Fez, greets or jokes with many we pass by. A world here, many worlds, and few who know or care about America. For a moment, I am overwhelmed by this mysterious knowledge: each of us a center, yet utterly peripheral.

> *Each face a riad*
> *holding a secret*
> *garden*

By mid-afternoon, we tell Rachad we are exhausted, have no need of yet another astonishing mosque, market, palace. Just a place to sit quietly, and talk. He's used to tourists manic in their desire to see everything, as though the calculus was only numerical. He shrugs, smiles, finds us two miniature wooden tables with chairs along a narrow, quiet alley. The man who runs the tiny café—who of course knows Rachad—brings green tea for Linda, a "Turkish coffee" for me, and savory muffins. We practice, it seems, the art of being in Morocco: gossip, about king and unruly children you're secretly proud of, what it means to be Berber, Arab, French, the allure and stain of colonial legacies, of university life in Europe, and the choice—for Rachad—to stay close to the home he was born to. Watch his teenagers navigate—like the tumultuous marketplace—a wild new world that comes, now, to their own doorstep.

> *A true guide leads you*
> *places you can't otherwise*
> *know*

As we walk the streets of Fez, Rachad answers a question about culture by pointing to the buildings themselves. The old Jewish Quarter, he says, has outward-facing balconies where life is lived communally in the streets, while Arab homes have interior-facing rooms opening onto private courtyards, where family life is lived *inside* the walls. New apartment complexes, he says, favor the outward-facing balconies of western life. Tall ones. Where, standing on the balcony you see only horizon, and inside, only yourself.

Intimacy depends on where
you look, and
how

WE'RE ON THE ROAD TO FATTAH'S HOUSE, a seven-hour drive along a modern highway. I am struck by both the familiarity of the landscape, and its utter foreignness. When I doze then wake, I could just as well be driving in California's great Central Valley. Then I see the Arabic-Berber road signs, or a mosque-turret rising from a village: reminders that I can't really know this Muslim world.

This *koan* of familiarity and strangeness occurs as I interact with Moroccans here: Lahcen and Mohammed, then Rachad, and the many friends of each guide in the towns we've walked through where, suddenly, everyone is just a human being, here on this planet. But then, one enters the leather tannery, or the tight, claustrophobic alleys of old town, and the faces become other worldly, or more-worldly than I'm used to seeing. Grizzled beards and gnarled hands of men hammering large brass bowls with their mallets, relentlessly; the aged cripple squatting each day, all day, for a coin; or the blind man, standing stoic as a statue in the dark alley holding a handful of blue cigarette packages for sale. But is this really unlike America? The poet Emma Lazarus famously wrote:

> Give me your tired, your poor, your huddled masses yearning to breathe free... send these, the homeless, tempest-tossed to me, I lift my lamp beside the golden door!

Yet our homeless are as bereft as any here. Still, I am swayed by the zestful antics of children, of teenage boys zooming by on scooters, the exuberance that seems irrepressible in human living wherever we land. The shopkeepers and hawkers and merchants so at home in their bodies, this ancient heritage, this Morocco.

> *My hand waves in wind*
> *out the van window*
> *like a flag*

Despite the delights of Morocco, Linda is a western woman in a medieval society, and is often incredulous. The hiddenness of a traditional woman's life, the proscribed limits of transit, appearance, gathering, compared with men who are everywhere visible. Even as a visiting male, I'm often asked what my wife might want, which is as inscrutable a question as there is. She doesn't laugh at this. I suspect the invisibility is even more acute for her since Moroccan women gather in their own spaces apart from prying western eyes. In the old villages anyway, over communal clothes-washing, the baking of bread, the selling of produce, often round a purposeful task—it becomes the real reason for lingering.

Even in the artisan shop where ceramics are made, men and women are divided by task, women painting the designs the men make because they are more "intuitive" with color, the men more linear. Or the comments from Lahcen about, say, the rare woman police officer who seems a strange novelty to him, about whom he says, "Well, you see they're the ones standing in the shade." To which I mischievously reply, "ah, they're the smart ones!"

> *To know your place and*
> *to have a place—wobbling*
> *rope bridge over*
> *chasm*

AT ANOTHER CAFÉ WITH RACHAD, I MINE HIM for stories over tea and bread. This time, about Morocco's relations with neighboring countries. He emphasizes cultural ties and economic exchanges that occur—post-colonial era—with France and Spain. The shared Andalusian history more binding than, say, the geographical ties with neighboring Algeria—which is problematic—or the north-African Mediterranean countries of Libya and Egypt. Apparently Tangiers, a small, close neighbor, has a certain cultural cache. But south, into and beyond the Sahara, is an Africa both foreign and distant. It's nuance I'm listening for:

the quizzical way Rachad holds the contrary nature of Morocco's history with the warp and weft of the Mediterranean. He smiles

recounting Morocco's existence as a "protectorate" when really, it was just another example of empire sweeping through this western outpost of Africa. Rachad sighs as he lifts his cup of tea, says that

one imagines Morocco as "Arabic," though Berbers like Rachad comprise 60% of the population and centuries ago saw the Arabs—like the Romans—as invaders. It's just that the Arabs stayed and intermarried with Berbers—as in his family—while the Romans left. And Moroccan Islam, originally the religion of invaders, grew roots. He places the empty cup on the wooden table again, savors the last crumbs of honey-bread. Says he loves all the strands of who he is. Like Moroccan *Amazigh* or Berber rugs, more beautiful *because* of the complex weave.

> *Tea dregs in an empty cup—*
> *calligraphy*

[*Warp and weft* are sometimes used in literature to describe the basic dichotomy of the world we live in, as in, up/down, in/out, black/white, Sun/Moon, yin/yang, etc. The expression is also used similarly for the underlying structure upon which something is built.]

[The little grains of tea or coffee left at the bottom of the cup are known as the *dregs*—the least wanted portion, or the residue. Though tea sediment is where extra nutrients and omens reside!]

IN THE VAN, WE ASK LAHCEN—OUR OMNIPRESENT DRIVER—what he thinks of the Moroccan king: the combined royal, political, religious, and military leader of the country. Lahcen sees him as a very good king, forward looking—unlike his father, who cared primarily for the royal family. The current king is the one responsible for extensive highway and road development, the placement of schools and clinics in towns throughout the countryside. The nature preserve we pass is another example, the long firebreaks in the hills to control wildfires—though now, as everywhere, climate change and drought threaten water supplies. But the "new" king is trying. Lahcen says this sincerely,

while the January 6th insurrection hearings unfold in America. The ugly specter of how close Trump came to a coup, how a country can turn on the whim of one man. So I have questions about what it's really like, here in Morocco, with so much power concentrated in a religious ruler that could turn oppressive by a simple temperamental change in its next ruler (who is now an eleven-year-old prince). It's still illegal to be gay, or publicly criticize the king in Morocco; though a bevy of similar rights in America erode even as I write this. Driving with Lahcen, I feel safe enough in this foreign country, for now; while my own teeters on the whims of a bully with fake orange hair.

> *Lahcen rolls down the window—*
> *free to say anything*
> *in the van*

DRIVING THE ENDLESS HIGHWAY, WE ANGLE into a rest stop for a cappuccino, cookie and kefir snacks, see an array of buildings with a bank, a pharmacy, a water park with a big swimming pool, a shooting range, even a McDonald's restaurant with its golden arches. The place is crowded, primarily with Moroccans. America, and the West, emulated here like empires of old. This country is more than any one thing. At the intersection on the way out,

the police stop a van with African immigrants, who Lahcen says migrate northward begging in the cities (not allowed in Morocco). Everywhere, it seems, this *koan* of immigrants attempting to find a safe place, anywhere, to call home.

>   *Who knows where any*
>   *of us will*
>   *end up*

AND THEN, THE DESERT VANISHES and the vast Atlantic looms on the horizon. We didn't realize we were heading west from Fez, so it's a delightful shock to see the vast blue of sea. "Keep going that way," Lahcen says, "and you'll find New York!" Which seems to impart a bit of the infinite to our conversation. Google maps, which wasn't operating in the barren spans of desert, now shows us traversing the Atlantic coast between Casablanca and the capitol Rabat. We'll head east now to Fattah's house, the ebullient musician and travel guru born not far from Marrakesh, whom we met in Santa Cruz at the Kuumbwa Jazz Center with his fusion band AZA. He lives in two worlds, and I'm not only talking about the spiritual and the material. His music is loved in Morocco, is one of the reasons Lahcen has become family. And in America, he has become an open door.

> *Fatah plays the banjo*
> *like a gimbri—*
> *this fusion of worlds*

Under the highway is a pedestrian tunnel from one stretch of stores to another. Even the brief dark a welcome respite from the sun. Lahcen opens the backdoor of the van upward, simply to stand in its shade. Once done with our browsing, we walk to the van past the gauntlet of young boys awaiting each commuter. Lahcen tells us not to encourage nor be intimidated by their insistence. Once in the van, having rejected each overture of Moroccan trinkets from the young boys, we smile and wave and they just can't help but lavish their smiles in return. Speaking French as though the whole world knew their tongue.

> *From the moon, Earth*
> *seems a tiny trinket*
> *you'd give your life for*

On the way to Fattah's house, Lahcen points to a hazy smudge of modern buildings on the horizon: the outskirts of Marrakesh. Too far to see the bulk of, just its dusty mirage. We meander instead through a small town of sprawling red-clay buildings, an impressive equestrian structure, and market after market of watermelons. Lahcen points out the large trucks taking watermelons to sell in other cities. But there's an underside to it all, he says: climate change, and the unregulated drilling of deep wells to facilitate irrigation projects for acre upon acre of watermelons. "The area used to be so green," Lahcen says—but now, entire fields of olive trees stand dead in their rows, due to the luscious watermelons, and lack of regulation. No one quite knows what will happen next, following this hidden red of sweet desire.

Green tattooed globes—
food of the desert gods

Fattah built his new home, Villa Ourti, in the small village of Ait Hadi southwest of Marrakesh. Right before the pandemic, and the blossoming of his Moroccan tours. Who knew? A spare desert walled in the traditional way, planted with new olive trees, a full garden, a deep well, a swimming pool, the house itself a "mini-palace" of two stories with multiple balconies looking toward the Atlas mountains. A western dollar goes a long way here.

Caretakers live in a small cottage on the grounds, look after the place when he's gone (like now, touring California)—when guests come, they cook delicious Moroccan meals, scatter red flowers on the bed. Lahcen lets his hair down here, too, as part of Fattah's "family"—sitting on the outdoor couches in his off-white *djellaba* chatting away with friends on the phone.

Fattah grew up in a village 20 kilometers from here; his wife's family lives nearby in the other direction. They have French connections, some living here, some there. Lahcen met Fattah ten years ago, became a driver for him because of his love of music. And family. As though they are the same thing.

> *I leave two books of poems*
> *to add to the music*
> *of Villa Ourti*

It is like waking inside a dream in this spacious white bedroom with red flower petals strewn on the sheets and floor, the French doors open to Moroccan desert, the sky silver-gray, the air cool. The previous *riad* in Fez was like the interior of a Tarot card, enclosed-in on itself like a puzzle of doors, stairways, windows facing the interior courtyard. Here, Fattah's Villa Ourti is everywhere open to the vast Moroccan desert, as though house and landscape are part of each other.

Over breakfast on the veranda, a tiny plump bird jumps from thin branch to thin branch in the modest lucky-nut tree next to me, eyeing my Moroccan bread and jam. The roosters crow on someone's farm nearby. Lahcen and our hosts banter in the kitchen in their Moroccan dialect that I am glad not to understand—without the complication of *meaning*, each syllable flows like bird-song, like water.

> *The art of being—*
> *this timeless*
> *practice*

I open Stephen Batchelor's *The Art of Solitude*, apropos for this day of contemplation in the wilds of Morocco. The excerpt, taken from an early Buddhist sutra, reminds me of imagery embodied in the hexagons my father built in the forests of Mariposa back home, and what they meant to him.

> *"Here is a fine hexagonal crystal..." So when her mind is collected, pure and bright...she understands: "This is my body, having physical form, composed of four elements, born of father and mother, nourished with rice and broth, impermanent, liable to be broken and destroyed, and this is my consciousness, supported by and bound up with it."*

The geometrical symbolism of Islamic architecture and calligraphy elicits a similar, deep resonance from my body. For this moment, to be a home for the infinite. It's a lovely surprise to find the hexagonal shape in ancient Buddhist scripture, Muslim art, and my father's memory. Meditation built into the very design of things.

> *The desert shimmers with*
> *the formless...*

EVEN IN MOROCCO, I BRING THE WORLD WITH ME in a book. While Lahcen relaxes with a coffee, I listen for how the desert evokes this *Art of Solitude*. Batchelor muses on this in Vermeer's work, and Agnes Martin's paintings.

> Johannes Vermeer and Agnes Martin both painted with their backs to the world. Whether surrounded by noisy children in a townhouse in Delft or alone on a mesa in the high desert of New Mexico, they pursued the same solitary vocation....
>
> To be alone at your desk or in your studio is not enough. You have to free yourself from the phantoms and inner critics who pursue you wherever you go. "When you start working," said the composer John Cage, "everybody is in your studio—the past, your friends, enemies, the art world, and above all, your own ideas—all are there. But as you continue painting, they start leaving, one by one, and you are left completely alone. Then, if you are lucky, even you leave."

I've always been drawn to solitude, even as a young boy, and now in the middle of Morocco, where the communal is omnipresent. Even Allah looks over your shoulder here. There is an art to maintaining one's fundamental solitude in the midst of village life. I know, for instance, if we had come on Fattah's previous tour with friends, these couches and patios would now be filled with chatter and conversation—lovely, I know. But Linda and I also have deep needs for solitude, and this tour where it's "just us" allows a more nuanced kind of pilgrimage. Lahcen looks up from his coffee, Linda comes to sit with us on the veranda. I close my book and listen.

> A diesel truck roars
> just outside
> the gate

Driving the endless desert in Morocco, one has time to think. I am seduced by the unitary culture built round the Five Pillars of Islam (which Lahcen says you don't have to be a zealot about). A beautiful mosque in every village and many in the big cities, the sense of belonging to a shared worldview, a communal Arabic-Berber culture. All set in the paternalistic landscape of a king—luckily, a good king at the moment—who can simply order the building of more highways and schools and hospitals. The daily lives of our guides, and the people they know in the cities and towns we stay in, seem relatively safe and orderly—it is a good life, if simple in economic terms for most (as in America).

Still, like this desert we drive through, it is a monochromatic world, with its latent dangers. Even for a tourist, homosexuality is outlawed, and you'd be scorned if too-flagrant in your affections with wife or husband. Though Moroccan men, particularly the old and young, often put their arms around each other, hold hands. There *is* a parliament, but it can be dissolved by the king if they are too contrary with him. A certain level of cultural and religious, and political, diversity is allowed here, but not too much. Most of the Jews have left. There aren't many Christian churches (perhaps understandable given centuries of religious war). It is an Islamic Berber-Arabic land, and everyone else is just visiting.

The haunting parallel for America is the conservative evangelical dream of returning to what Morocco has: a theocracy. This morning, I'd read the Texan Republican platform vows to re-establish a Christian nation with many of the unitary cultural mores that Morocco has. And in a worse-case scenario, edging into dystopian visions of *The Handmaid's Tale*, or more historically, the realities of life during the Spanish Inquisition and similar tests of purity. This is America after all—we like to excel at everything.

> *Nothing moves in the desert*
> *except the mind*

IN THE VAN, I MOVE TO THE FRONT SEAT to chat with Lahcen. It's a long road from here to there. I ask him what he thinks of America, but it is too far away to take seriously. He considers it a place where you can have whatever you want, like a cell phone. Which he can now get in Morocco. I muse that America must again offer some unifying national sense of belonging beyond consumerism and capitalism to be satisfying to its own populace. Even the best shopper wants, deep down, something more than *stuff*. Lahcen is silent for a long spell. *Freedom* is the word that eventually comes. But for what purpose, I say aloud. We drive in silence again. It's a long road from here to there.

The adhan echoes from the mosque:
prayer is better than sleep.

[The Muslim call to morning prayer, or *adhan*: the first phrase is said four times and the rest twice. *Ashhadu an la ilaha illa Allah*—I bear witness that there is no god except the One God. *Assalatu khairum-minan-naum*—Prayer is better than sleep.]

We wake to cold, gray skies at Fattah's, late June, even here in Morocco. Over breakfast with Lahcen—coffee, fruit, bread and honey—we chat about the Moroccan police. He is matter-of-fact regarding the omnipresence of both uniformed and anonymous police, who check on the whereabouts of every foreigner visiting each day. Hotels and riads provide the visa-stamp number, and on day-trips such as we did yesterday to Essaouira, the police ask drivers like Lahcen how long we're staying, where are we going next. Ostensibly to keep the country free from terrorists, and to keep the precious tourism business going without costly disruption. I remember years before in Bali, the airport bombing that destroyed the island's tourist livelihood—you become wary of the unexpected. Still, it's a little eerie:

authority. You can sense Lahcen's careful, respectful attitude toward the police during any encounter. He doesn't want me mistaken for an infidel who'd carry a bomb in my black backpack, rather than a blank notebook, the fuse of words burning their way into a poem.

> *Lahcen shrugs—happy*
> *to keep me safe*
> *enough*

BREAKFAST CAN TAKE A LONG TIME AT FATTAH'S, in the desert, on the veranda, with no place in particular to go on our rest day. Endless baked breads, Moroccan tea, the fruit succulent. Wind in the olive trees. I ask Lahcen about journalism,

to what extent newspapers and other media outlets can report on what they want. He laughs as he scrolls his smart-phone for entertainment and news. Says the main taboo is against saying anything bad about the king and the royal family. You don't do that, in Morocco. If you want to remain free. But other complaints can be made or issues reported without undue blowback, except, as Lahcen says, from one's own family and community. It's all very tightly-knit here. Say something grumpy about a relative, and there can be hell to pay. Or announce a wedding—suddenly the world shows up to celebrate. I laugh too,

spread more honey on my *barbari* bread, but complain about the opposite in America. You can shout any damn thing you like, and few seem to care. Families, too, are spread so far it's difficult to stay in touch. Lahcen considers this as he sips his tea. Both of us uncertain, for a moment, about who has the better deal.

Moroccan tea—
gunpowder rolled

[Gunpowder tea: each leaf is individually rolled into a small pellet. When you steep, each individual leaf unrolls or "explodes." The tea tastes lightly smoky—as the name indicates.]

As we drive to Marrakech, Linda leans over and says she wants to remember these images from our daily travels:

> *Boys riding mules laden with astonishing amounts of straw or rugs or random items piled higher than you'd imagine.*
>
> *Shepherds dressed in long hooded-cloaks to protect from sun, standing in sparse fields watching their sheep.*
>
> *Carts everywhere decorated with red tassels and colorful embroidery. Some pulled by mules, others pushed by men. The engines of commerce.*
>
> *Large cargo trucks carrying propane tanks, or watermelons, in all directions.*
>
> *In the villages, men gather hoping to be picked for various work projects. The streets often filled with the detritus of business and packaging. and personal items—there's no systematic ways of keeping the roads and countryside clean.*
>
> *Everywhere, the business of making a living in the desert. Vast fields of agriculture, or small farm plots. New stone walls surround vacant rock fields waiting for a house or an orchard—and of course, waiting for water.*

From the van, I can become a *jenn* spirit, secreting myself in the lives of each boy, shepherd, mule. Even the crippled cart, the broken watermelons ripe with red stories and black seeds.

> *Deep underground—*
> *the muse of*
> *water*

[In Morocco, spirits occupy a prominent position in the popular imagination. They are commonly known as *jnun* (sing. *jenn*) for the males and *jenniyat* (sing. *jenniya*) for the females. Lots of Moroccans, if not all, hold a firm belief in *jnun*.]

On the road to Marrakesh, the goats balanced in trees by their shepherds make a poem. One solely devoted to them. A score of goats in each tree, small hooves perched on each limb capable of bearing their weight. Unmoving, stoic. A tragic fall just an inch either way. Six or seven trees in a row. Lahcen, our guide and driver, doesn't like the gimmick, performed for a few coins from locals and Europeans alike. But who knows the mind of a goat? They'll eat anything, and perhaps crave new experiences. Like tourists. Only their shepherd can perch them high enough to see the Atlas mountains in the distance. The smallest goats, the luckiest—perched near the crown. The land now like a map of the everything you could eat if only you could.

> *By day's end, the goats are happy*
> *to find earth*
> *again*

Arriving in Marrakech is a revelation, a shock, a bombshell after the open desert of Fattah's. Immense new hotel and mall complexes, noisy traffic, scooters, pedestrians—a Moroccan tumult. We pick up our guide for the day, Saïd—another longtime friend of Fattah's—and make our way to the Jardin Majorelle, a garden and museum in the memory of the French painter Jacques Majorelle (1886-1962).

> *The Majorelle Garden (French: Jardin Majorelle, Arabic:* حديقة ماجوريل *hadiqat mmajuril; Berber languages: urti majuril) is a one-hectare botanical and artist's landscape garden. Created by the artist Jacques Majorelle over almost forty years, starting in 1923, it features a Cubist villa designed by the French architect, Paul Sinoir. The property was the residence of the artist and his wife for a quarter-century. In the 1980s, it was purchased by the fashion designers, Yves Saint-Laurent and Pierre Bergé who worked to restore it. Today, the garden and villa complex is open to the public. The villa houses the Berber Museum and in 2017 the Yves Saint Laurent Museum opened nearby.*

This strange lineage of colonial and indigenous cultures mixing in memory. The garden, lush with water from the Atlas Mountains, the tall bamboo and green foliage creating shade against the hot Marrakech sun. The Berber tribal artifacts, clothing, jewelry are striking, and one can picture these women and men fiercely clothed in beauty before Arab then French peoples brought their own. It's not only blood, but art that carries the day. The museum, now, a synesthesia of peoples and time. The final display set under a dome of virtual night-sky twinkling with stars—quite the effect in this heat. Almost real.

> *Saïd says he still*
> *wonders*

WE DISCOVER THAT OUR GUIDES—MOHAMMED, RACHAD, the omnipresent Lahcen, and now Saïd—are why we came to Morocco. The stories, more than the mosques we dare not trespass. The ordinary intimacies as much as the blue walls of Chefchaouen, even the savory tagine meals simmered in red clay. Saïd tries his best all day, but we confess, finally, that we are exhausted. He finds another perfect café, like previous guides, with a small lacquered table and chairs on a quiet alley (our small vice), and engage in marvelous dialogue with Saïd about his life, his children, his sense of Morocco, his curiosity about Americans. This, more than any additional glimpses into the mad marketplaces, is what we'll remember.

> *He's been a tourist guide for 25 years, lives now outside of the city where its quieter with his wife and three children. He used to conduct tours all over Morocco, but tends now to focus on Marrakech in order to be close to his teenage children. Says they need him more now.*
>
> *Saïd has a Master's degree in European Literature, wrote his dissertation on Bertolt Brecht, the German theatre practitioner, playwright, and poet. He was taken by Brecht's theme that it is in the communal, not just the individual, that humans find their way.*

I share one of my favorite writers, Dr. Irvin Yalom's existential notion that we exist *because* we live in the tensions between our need for separateness and belongingness, both. Morocco is such a communal country, I say, bound together by bonds of language, tribe, religion. Ask what it's like to feel the West seeping in at every turn? We consider this over more tea,

hear the call of the *self*, echoing between us like new prayer. Saïd sees it in his own children, though his wife just shrugs. *What are parents to do?* Or a country, for that matter.

> *Any fundamentalist has the*
> *answer, sharpened*
> *like a blade*

A LAST EVENING IN MARRAKECH—WE WANDER THE MARKETS on our own, look for a place to eat. Find a modest café on a side street near the square where we can people-watch over dinner. A simple meal of grilled chicken and vegetable skewers, supplemented generously by our amiable young host who brings us free slices of watermelon from the back of a diesel truck full of ripe green globes. The melons will go bad in the Moroccan heat, so at the end of the day what remains is shared, split open by blade or ground. He offers the wet red flesh with a flourish, the juice watering our tongues.

Communion–
in Marrakech

THE DRIVE TO CASABLANCA TAKES NEARLY THREE HOURS through now-familiar landscapes akin to Mars or Utah. The drive into the heart of the city adds more delays through gnarled urban traffic. But the sight of the Hassan II Mosque is worth the trouble. An immense edifice sitting astride a grand plaza on the edge of the Atlantic sea, both mosque and courtyards can hold tens of thousands of worshipers.

> The Hassan II Mosque (Arabic: مسجد الحسن الثاني; French: Grande Mosquée Hassan II) is the second largest functioning mosque in Africa, and the 7th largest in the world. Its minaret is the world's second tallest at 689 feet. Completed in 1993, it was designed by Michel Pinseau under the guidance of King Hassan II and built by Moroccan artisans from all over the kingdom. The minaret is 60 stories high topped by a laser, the light from which is directed towards Mecca. The walls are of hand-crafted marble and the roof is retractable—105,000 worshippers can gather together for prayer: 25,000 inside the mosque hall and another 80,000 on the mosque's outside ground.

It is the only Moroccan mosque open to non-Muslims, as though saying *Look at all you're missing*. Or, *Size matters*. We buy tickets, are ushered with other English speakers inside, each language group with its own translator. The soaring spaces defy description even for a poet, or a tour guide. Pictures from the internet, or taken with my own camera, do the mosque injustice. Domes, minarets, arches, gleaming marble at every turn—as though a race of dinosaurs or tall gods lived here. We roam—under tight surveillance—like gawkers, heads tilted back, tongues lolling. Still,

it has little of the *welcoming* most Catholic cathedrals provide where any can enter, sit, pray, or wander its beauty (at least before the pandemic). Of course Protestant churches—the lifeblood I grew up on—provide neither entry nor much beauty except during scheduled services. Mosques, while omnipresent in every Moroccan village and city, can be viewed only from the outside unless one is a true believer. Like the *medinas* and *riads*, Muslim society is turned secretly toward the inside of itself. Which is an unnerving experience for outsiders. Especially Americans, who can treat the world like a bed and breakfast, order whatever we want. Be miffed when disappointed. Write a scathing review.

> *No one can stop me*
> *from loving all*
> *I see*

Portugal & Spain, Again

After Morocco, the Lisbon airport in Portugal feels oddly like home, and we, comfortable again in its European demeanor. Even the Portuguese signage, which is still undecipherable, looks familiar-enough after more than a week of Arabic and Berber.

We order an Uber which comes within five minutes, takes us cross town to our B&B in Belém, just north of Lisbon proper. The friendly driver named Tiago is a young man sporting a luxurious Peugeot with a sky-roof extending the full length of the car. Quite the way to see the Lisbon skyline, and the stars above, as we drive through an extensive tree-lined hillside to our flat. After twelve hours of travel from Marrakech, feeling now like royalty,

it all collapses when deposited late at night on a dark street with no one to greet us. Battered trash cans line the narrow front yard. A flickering Barber sign vaguely lights one of the closed ground floor apartments. *Where in the world are we?* Grumpy and bone-weary, we finally get hold of our young host who'd been busy checking-in another party elsewhere. Eventually, we haul our luggage up the stairs to a bohemian student pad with thin French doors open to a tiny rusted porch, opening, he says, to a hidden botanical garden across the street. "It's like Eden," he encourages us—and with no exit but exhausted sleep, we almost believe.

*The flickering light
is a sign*

This morning, Linda is up early exploring the neighborhood on our first day in Belém. Brings back coffee, tea and Portuguese pastries. We'll find a grocery store later, but are happy to simply sit for a spell in our funky flat with the battered French doors, look at the dense trees of the hidden botanical garden across the street. Is this how Eve and Adam felt, after paradise sported an iron gate? Eons later,

we *are* this intrepid couple exploring a Belém made possible only by their flight into this chaos of world. Grudgingly, I offer a prayer of thanks to them. I think I'm tired. We're here for four days before heading to Seville, Spain. America is only a chimera now, we've been away so long. Travel a kind of Zen *koan*, revealing one's original face before a country gave you one.

> *A peacock screech–*
> *hint of the garden*

BELÉM IS A FREGUESIA (CIVIL PARISH) OF LISBON, the capital of Portugal. We wanted to be on the outskirts, but still in the middle of everything. Early evening, we walk toward the Tagus riverfront, which mimics an immense bay before emptying into the Atlantic. Different than the teeming Moroccan medinas we've come from—back in Europe with its now-familiar Western contours. Asphalt streets, cement curbs, glass windows, grocery and department stores. Not a mule in sight. Which is funny, since Portugal initially seemed so foreign to us. Now, the world is more intimate and strange at the same time. The ocular gyrations of consciousness that travel engenders. Suddenly,

we hear a haunting rendition of Joni Mitchell's "A Case of You" sung by a woman hidden somewhere up the stone parapet we walk by. Entranced, we detour up an alley looking for the concert, find instead a fundraiser for the school that the beautiful old building turns out to be. Hovering parents, children cavorting, the singer who makes this world, suddenly, so intimate.

This folk song also
a call to prayer

Along the sprawling riverfront of Belém, we are confronted by the immense colonial colossus Monument of the Discoveries, stuck like a beacon of past empire, pointed like an arrow out the Atlantic at worlds known and unknown. Almost naked in its *suchness*, when conquering was still considered noble.

> *Padrão dos Descobrimentos is located along the river where ships departed to explore and trade with India, the Orient, and beyond—celebrating the Portuguese Age of Discovery during the 15th and 16th centuries. Sculpted in the form of a ship's prow, dozens of figures from Portuguese history follow a statue of Henry the Navigator sculpted in bas-relief. Adjacent to the monument is a calçada square in the form of a map, showing the routes of various Portuguese explorers during the Age of Discovery.*

Even here in Portugal, there are indigenous history reformations brewing, pushing for a more frank picture of what it was like to "discover" worlds already civilized for eons. War, genocide and its conceits. I stand directly in front of the towering prow, stare up at the figure of Henry far above whose own sight is set on the distant horizon. He is beautiful. He is dangerous. He is likely one of the reasons I can even visit across the seas. The globe so intimate now as to make him blush.

There is no end
to horizon

WE WALK TO AN ASTONISHING MONASTERY IN BELÉM, another chance to entertain my "past life flashback" as a monk or scholar in such architecturally sacred environs. Where do these flights of fancy come from? Bone memory? Metaphysical hubris? How many lives does one person want? I take many photos, because the angles of sun on the stone masonry in the three-story courtyard is endlessly varied, with deep blue sky and differing white clouds framing each shot.

> The Jerónimos Monastery or Hieronymites Monastery is a former monastery of the Order of Saint Jerome near the Tagus river in the parish of Belém, Portugal. The monastery is one of the most prominent examples of the Portuguese Late Gothic Manueline style of architecture in Lisbon. It was classified a UNESCO World Heritage Site, and houses the tomb of Fernando Pessoa.

Ah, Pessoa! I almost missed him, not having read the monastery's history before entering. Walking the medieval balconies rimming the courtyard, he suddenly appears in an alcove: the tomb of Fernando Pessoa, whose *Book of Disquiet* accompanies me while traveling this Andalusian terrain. If there was a man who understood the psyche as a multiplicity, harboring many discrete lives within one body, it is Fernando. His remains were moved here fifty years after his death at the Hospital de São Luís. The memorial is a single, elegant, tall rectangle of marble:

TOMB OF FERNANDO PESSOA

> One of the most important Portuguese poets of the 20th century.
>
> He embodied several literary personalities, such as—Alberto Caeiro, Ricardo Reis and Álvaro de Campos. His body was transferred to this monastery on the 50th anniversary of his death.

Reincarnation is not a necessary conceit. But the imagination is, as Pessoa knows. He tells me the monks are a little stuffy, here, but the parade of visitors is refreshing. Especially in death.

> *Stone gargoyles wink—*
> *a dead man still*
> *sings*

In Portugal, as elsewhere, it's easy to romanticize a writer's life. Pessoa's life was his own, lived in these everyday streets. Pessoa's assets: this chest, with more than 25,000 pages, and part of his personal library. Yet I'm reminded of the perils of living for a book, as a book—though it is a noble life.

At a small café in Belém, I read an interview with Ocean Vuong in a Buddhist magazine musing on the impermanence of literature and life..

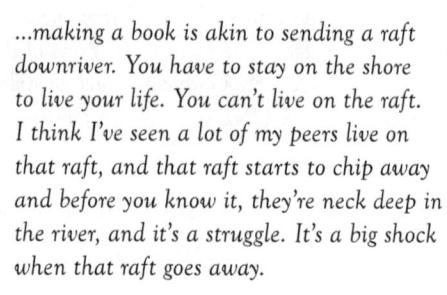

> ...making a book is akin to sending a raft downriver. You have to stay on the shore to live your life. You can't live on the raft. I think I've seen a lot of my peers live on that raft, and that raft starts to chip away and before you know it, they're neck deep in the river, and it's a struggle. It's a big shock when that raft goes away.
>
> And so for me, there has to be a difference between living and making. You make something, you send it downriver, but you have to stay on the steady ground of the shore.

That said...I love this.

The dark cappuccino on my wood table is its own alphabet, its delirious life. This tiny corner of street high above the Tagus River. As a writer, I hope to disbelieve the lines of my own narrative. The impossibility of living a life less real than it is.

> *I am a book—of bone,*
> *raft, and river*

We spend an afternoon in the Jardim Botanico Tropical gardens we can see an edge of through our tiny front balcony in Belém. It's part of a larger palace complex closed for restoration, but it's the garden we love. Walk the immense palm-rimmed grounds created for a 1940 world fair.

> The Portuguese World Exhibition (Exposição do Mundo Português) was held in Lisbon in 1940 to mark 800 years since the foundation of the country and 300 years since the restoration of independence from Spain. The fair was held on the Praça do Império, and attended by 3 million people.

The grounds retain their beautiful ponds and peacocks, an array of tropical and native trees and plants. We wander, sit, write. There's an old Portuguese-Chinese display, falling into ruin, an odd mix of Asian-styled gardens with Portuguese elements—which of course means Andalusian, too. Which means Arab, and suddenly the world is a tangled mycelial web of cultures and peoples—like a family. Still, the regal busts of a pair of African figures—a man and woman—that were part of a "colonial exhibition" are placed at multiple spots throughout the park. Beautiful, decaying. Naked colonialism—celebrated at the 1940 exhibition—now a poignant reminder of the past. It's too much

to understand. But while the arches and sculptures of a previous era erode, the lush trees renew themselves—with a little tending—and the peacocks make more peacocks and *Nature* herself whispers secrets to us beneath language.

> *This garden is more*
> *than a garden*

Interlude: A Map of the Path So Far

Ah, the pilgrimage of travel, with its Pessoa-like tedium and epiphanies. Yet here we are on the "sixth stage" of our journey in Sevilla, Spain. For Linda, her seventh (depending on how you count): the Camino, then meeting-up in Santiago, Spain for several days; a train to Porto, Portugal for a two-week stay; a plane to Lisbon for a couple days; the flight to Morocco for nine days; a return to Lisbon in the Belem district for four more days; then today's flight here, to Sevilla.

Seville is another fascinating intersection for tribal, Roman, Islamic, Christian, Jewish cultures, the emergence of a unique Spanish empire, then smaller country, now a key member of the European Union. We didn't even get our passports checked or go through customs when landing in Spain from Portugal—and the currency of course is now the same. But this one small region has been on its own pilgrimage for millennia.

> Seville; Spanish: Sevilla, is the capital and largest city of the Spanish autonomous community of Andalusia and the province of Seville. It is situated on the lower reaches of the River Guadalquivir, in the southwest of the Iberian Peninsula.
>
> Its old town contains three World Heritage Sites: the Alcázar palace complex, the Cathedral, and the General Archive of the Indies. The Seville harbour, located 50 miles from the Atlantic Ocean, is the only river port in Spain.
>
> Seville was founded as the Roman city of Hispalis. Known as Ishbiliyah after the Islamic conquest in 711, Seville became the centre of the independent Taifa of Seville following the collapse of the Caliphate of Córdoba in the early 11th century; later it was ruled by Almoravids and Almohads until being incorporated to the Crown of Castile in 1248. Owing to its role as gateway of the Spanish Empire's trans-atlantic trade, managed from the Casa de Contratación, Seville became one of the largest cities in Western Europe in the 16th century. Coinciding with the Baroque period, the 17th century in Seville represented the most brilliant flowering of the city's culture; then began a gradual decline as silting in the Guadalquivir River forced the trade monopoly to relocate to the nearby port of Cádiz.

The 20th century in Seville saw the tribulations of the Spanish Civil War, decisive cultural milestones such as the Ibero-American Exposition of 1929 and Expo '92, and the city's election as the capital of the Autonomous Community of Andalusia.

I like the idea of a city, a region, a country being on its own pilgrimage. One that takes, not days, but millennia.

> *The never-ending story*
> *of us*

OF COURSE, THEN WE ARRIVE—FAMOUS PERSONAGES, apparently, caught by roaming paparazzi seducing tourists to think we are more than we are. Or less, if we don't buy the story...

*The newspaper flutters
in the young photographer's
hand*

Looking for our rental flat in Sevilla, the Google map initially leaves us stranded on the wrong street. The entrance to the Plaza de la Alianza is tucked behind a maze of old-town buildings where its courtyard waits like an oasis. Just around the corner from the immense Catedral de Seville, yet shielded from the tourist hullabaloo. Astonishing, how sound disappears round the old stone. In the green doorway

is one of the two "Barbaras" we know to be our hosts, standing like a Spanish elf at the threshold. Our new home for five days. She ushers us upstairs to a modest adobe-pink colored flat, shows us each nook and cranny, then spreads a map of the city across the table. We know no Spanish, and she little English—but her spry eyes and nimble hands direct us across the maze of avenues and alleys with love, trusting we too will fall under Sevilla's spell. To love a city is to care for the world. To welcome strangers—a prayer that needs no translation.

> *Cathedral bells ring—*
> *penetrating every*
> *wall*

First full morning in Sevilla. I wake slowly in our flat while Linda walks early. The church bells toll loudly as though we're inside the cathedral itself. Yet, so seductive: I wouldn't think of covering my ears. It's time to delve back into my Andalusian writers, so a bit of Lorca this morning, with his ecstatic melancholy:

> The Great Sadness
>
> *You can't look at yourself*
> *in the ocean.*
> *Your looks fall apart*
> *like tendrils of light.*
> *Night on earth.*

From *The Return*

> *I'm coming back*
> *for my wings.*

An American is ever suspicious of melancholy, as though it is the great failure. In Spain, it seems the secret to living—how else to fall in love with night and moon. In music and the literature of dream, to find again the nub of lost wings.

> *Lorca sings to me like*
> *the Great Friend*

THIS SMALL FLAT IN SEVILLA HAS TWO LARGE DOUBLE-WINDOWS opening to the courtyard below. Over coffee and an obscene *churros con chocolate*, I wonder how Andalusian poets could ever be unhappy. Though dark chocolate itself is enigmatic metaphor for soul and its delicious mourning. This pilgrimage

is both mirror and window. Looking outside, I also see inside. And Spain, well, I'll catch only a glimmer while straining to glimpse her soul. It's worth the failure. I read Pessoa again, his litany of soul lost in its own unknowing, waking up—as I imagine—in a post-Catholic world turning modern, looking for some mooring, finding none, and secretly wanting the terror of it.

> *Like someone on a hill who tries to make out the people in the valley, I look down at myself from on high, and I'm a hazy and confused landscape, just like everything else...*
>
> *I feel as if I'm always on the verge of waking up. I'm oppressed by the very self that encases me, asphyxiated by conclusions...*
>
> *I'm like someone searching at random, not knowing what object he's looking for nor where it was hidden. We play hide-and-seek with no one. There's a transcendent trick in all of this, a fluid divinity we can only hear.*

In this I feel the thread of Zen's *not-knowing is most intimate*, rather than any catholic certainty about what world and soul are. Andalusia reminds me of all I don't know, the enigmatic past, the opaque future. This *presence* the only arbiter of either, with its tiny mirrors and windows. I wash my cup, sweep crumbs into the bin. Put Pessoa into my backpack, and Lorca, just in case I need them when walking the streets of Sevilla.

> *The moon has no history,*
> *the wind never knows*
> *where next*
> *it will*
> *go*

So, Seville, Sevilla...like a new date, I want to know her name, her aliases, what she calls herself. Flattered, she laughs as I flip pages looking for the love in language itself. She is many things.

> *Hisbaal is the oldest name for Seville, originating with the Phoenician colonization of the Tartessian culture in south-western Iberia. It refers to the god Baal.*
>
> *According to Manuel Pellicer Catalán, the ancient name was Spal, meaning "lowland" in the Phoenician language (cognate to the Hebrew Shfela and the Arabic Asfal (أسفل). During Roman rule, the name was Latinized as Hispal and later as Hispalis. After the Umayyad invasion, this name remained in use among the Mozarabs, being adapted into Arabic as Išbīliya (إشبيلية).*
>
> *In the meantime, the city's official name had been changed to Ḥimṣ al-Andalus (حمص الأندلس), in reference to the city of Homs in modern Syria, the 'jund' Seville had been assigned to upon the Umayyad conquest; Ḥims al-Andalus remained an affectionate name for the city during the whole period throughout the Muslim Arab world. The city is sometimes referred to as the Pearl of Andalusia.*

Sevilla likes being a pearl in someone's eye, though her heart is not so easily given. Besides, I am faithless, will leave in a handful of days, though she has many lovers. All she wants, it seems, is to remain mysterious. Let's me kiss her hand.

> *Each iris holds*
> *a black hole,*
> *infinite*

Roaming Seville, I find the *Archivo de Indies* [Archive of the Indies], "the most important archive in the world containing records of the government and administration of the New World during the Spanish colonization." It's a building, and a record, embodying much pride for Spanish civic culture—the dimly lit halls towering with mosaics and marble, artifacts, the sweep of history. The most eerie might be centuries-old ledgers, inventories of gold, land, slaves. As though Nazis had won, curating their own holocaust museums as beacons of triumph. Still, I know it is more than tragedy or triumph:

almost like a mother, feral, ferocious, this curation of history. Because after, I spend a long spell inside the Royal Alcazar, a walled palace just around the corner from our flat, a sprawling blend of Muslim and Christian architecture that belies the fierce wars embedded in its walls. The gardens are immense, with colorful murals, fountains, hedges and walkways occupying acres. Here, where one world becomes another over and again. Till the art of contraries is all that remains.

> *From a distance,*
> *all flags look*
> *the same*

The bells of the Sevilla Cathedral ring out early—our little flat is part of its sound, given the proximity. We, too, are a bell. The neighborhood rhythmically bursts into life, then is silent, as residents and patrons come and go. The grizzled artist next door was up late last night, entertaining young people amid his paintings in the courtyard. This morning, he won't open his studio till late—despite the bells, which are ringing again—which is how the time goes here. *Awake! Awake! Awake!*

> *The grumpy artist sleeps*
> *all morning, awake*
> *in dream*

AFTER SO MANY DAYS OF TRAVEL, MY BRAIN AND BODY sometimes float in a kind of fog. So much to see, will we miss anything important, how to get beneath the surface of a city? We'll be busy sight-seeing later, so I enjoy these solitary minutes before. Flip through Lorca's poems rather than travel guides, find this:

The Garden

*was never born, never,
but could burst into life.*

*Every moment it's
deepened, restored.
Every moment it opens new
unheard-of pathways.*

*Over here! over there!
See my multiple bodies..*

*Everything open! Locks
to fit every key...*

*Here I'll mull over all
I once could have been.
God or beggar,
water or old marguerite.*

*My multiple paths
barely stained
now form this enormous rose
encircling my body.*

*Like an impossible map
the garden of the possible
every moment is
deepened, restored...*

And with that, I am ready. An enormous rose encircling my body. An impossible map to guide me through this garden of the possible. This city and its multiple bodies. *Over here! Over there! Everything open!*

> *A city is like a lover
> pining for your
> affection*

HERE, IN THE MIDST OF RELIGIOUS ARCHITECTURE and tantalizing art was the very seat of power and finance that animated Sevilla, and the Spanish empire. Yet it's not here anymore—it's all just memory, beauty, and pathos. The halls of modern power and finance lie elsewhere in Spain—as it often does in old landmark cities—in skyscrapers on the edge of things. Edifices that no one visits for beauty or pathos. Just entertainment, and shopping. Yet it surrounds this old world on all sides. I prefer

a cathedral to just be a cathedral: ancient stone, light, bells. Politicians drifting to the edges. The king nowhere in sight.

Circling the old city:
taxis—envoys
from a new
world

We walk round the corner from our flat to tour the Seville Cathedral, and the adjacent Giralda Tower. What an extravaganza! The interior so large it is divided into discrete worship areas with their own statuary, paintings, wooden benches. We are like fish in the stream of history, or birds tracing the magnetic arcs of migration.

> The Cathedral of Saint Mary of the See (Spanish: Catedral de Santa María de la Sede), better known as Seville Cathedral, is a Roman Catholic cathedral in Andalusia, Spain. It is a World Heritage Site, along with the adjoining Alcázar palace complex and the General Archive of the Indies. It is the fourth-largest church in the world (its size remains a matter of debate) as well as the largest Gothic church.
>
> After its completion in the early 16th century, Seville Cathedral supplanted Hagia Sophia in Istanbul as the largest cathedral in the world, a title the Byzantine church had held for a thousand years. Its royal chapel holds the remains of the city's conqueror Ferdinand III of Castile, his son and heir Alfonso the Wise and their descendant king Peter the Just. Christopher Columbus and his son Diego are also buried in the cathedral.

Christopher and his son are both buried here—a poignant bit of history. As the story goes, the Italian explorer didn't want to be buried on the Spanish soil that funded his journey across the sea, so his coffin is held aloft by immense stone pallbearers, marching into the center of the cathedral. He'd asked to be buried in the Americas, but no church of sufficient stature existed there. Now, few would have him. Which is the way of fame and infamy. I stare

at his marble coffin, wonder what it is he saw. There on the horizon. A continent that shouldn't be there. Forests of people, in the way.

> *The pallbearers stare*
> *straight ahead, never*
> *arriving*

FINALLY, IT IS TIME TO ESCAPE HISTORY—MUSEUMS, cathedrals—so we make our getaway. It all merits more angst and wonder, of course—being in the belly of the far-flung Spanish empire in its day—but the tourist pushes the pilgrim aside and wants to eat.

We walk to a restaurant Linda had seen reviewed, Bodega Santa Cruz, for exquisite tapas—chicken, pork, rice with savory vegetables—and beer that seems a kind of eucharist in the heat of day.

I suspect much of history is unrecorded: sitting, like this, over food and drinks. Ignoring the clerics. Hiding from marauders. Preferring festival over war. The closest I may ever come to understanding it all: honey-hued ale, this flesh of the wild world.

The siren call of ordinary days:
abandon ship,
sing

Two more days in Sevilla before we transit to Barcelona. Our courtyard alive with birds and children, the rhythmic presence of cathedral bells, the staccato drill-and-saw of workmen in the plaza. We've been traveling Portugal, Morocco, and Spain for five weeks now. And I am still keeping company with Andalusian writers like Federico Garcia Lorca, as good a travel guide as I'll find. This morning, we have a conversation. He says,

> *Every step we take on earth*
> *brings us to a new world.*
> *Every foot supported*
> *on a floating bridge.*
>
> *And I know that there is no*
> *straight road in this world—*
> *only a giant labyrinth*
> *of intersecting crossroads.*
>
> *And steadily our feet*
> *keep walking & creating*
> *—like enormous fans—*
> *these roads in embryo.*
>
> *Oh garden of white*
> *theories! garden*
> *of all I am not, all*
> *I could & should have been!*

[From Lorca's "Floating Bridges"]

There is no straight road in this world I repeat back to him, and he seems surprised. You never know with tourists, he says—they prefer the most direct route, especially ones that fancy themselves pilgrims. I tell him my plan for the day: *Walking and creating—like enormous fans—these roads in embryo.* Plagiarism, he says, is the best way to honor a poet. He smiles, if you can call it a smile, then dissolves into my book (well, *his* book) and gets comfortable in the bottom of my black backpack. It could be an interesting day.

> *Spain—poets everywhere*
> *like leaves,*
> *rustling*

THE ARTIST WHOSE STUDIO IS ADJACENT THE COURTYARD is in iconic form. He's a painting in himself, old but handsome, smoking, full of rumbling pathos, voice echoing into the plaza with every small eruption. Entering his studio, I browse the work of twenty artists in the collective, can tell his world is here—has little to do with America or the English language or anything happening on the continent of my birth. I find this deeply satisfying. He seems a dreamer, gritty yet full of sky and dark clouds. His eyes almost surprised to see something similar in me. How can this be? Americans usually want to buy art, not become it. We discuss—or did we—Pessoa's *Book of Disquiet*.

> *Seeing is perhaps a form of dreaming, but if we call it seeing instead of dreaming, it's so we can distinguish between the two.*
>
> *But what good are these speculations in linguistic psychology? Independently of me the grass grows, the rain falls on the grass that grows, the hills have been there for ages, and the wind blows in the same way as when Homer heard it, even if he didn't exist.*

"Surrealism," he says, "is pretending we're having a longer conversation than we are, with Pessoa too." I am almost desperate to find even one painting to buy, but there are none as handsome as he. So he goes back to smoking in the courtyard, while I climb the stairs to our second story flat. Both of us happy, it seems, for dream.

> *The glow of his cigarette—*
> *fire in the dark*
> *lighting the*
> *way*

We head cross-city through Sevilla's winding streets, aim for shade-filled quiet alleys rather than the rumble of urban avenues. It is blistering. Our destination: the Mushroom.

> *Standing in the Plaza de la Encarnación is Metropol Parasol, also known as the "mushrooms of Seville" ("Las Setas de Sevilla"). The building was designed by the German architect Jürgen Mayer, who won a design competition to revitalize the square. It is the largest wooden construction in the world (150 x 70 meters and 26 meters in height). Mayer won the competition partly thanks to the way he integrated the remains of a newly discovered Roman colony into his building. People originally wanted to build a parking lot here, but that was abandoned when Roman remains were discovered.*

The old world just beneath the new. Traversing the towering curved walkways with ample views of Sevilla, I think it a marriage between Marriott's Great America and a modern art museum. Unique—and while we sit below in the shade of the thing after, it becomes a postmodern cathedral: soaring spaces, more Arabic than Christian in its spare geometries, and absent the tortured histories of, say, Queen Isabella and Christopher Columbus, just to name two. I love the mushroom. The shade. The absence of history. Except for the bones of Romans.

> *The lowly mushroom—*
> *soaring now in*
> *space*

The Seville weather edges toward 100 degrees, so as we walk the shaded side of streets toward the Mercado de Feria, the oldest market dating back to the 18th century. Our B&B host, Barbara, says this is a "must" for genuine Spanish seafood, and it is quite the fish-haunt indeed. The Cantina restaurant hugs a rear corner of the larger market, shaded and misted, but is a calamity of gawking patrons waiting to be seated at the scatter of outdoor tables. Discerning there might be a list, we find the maestro of this cacophony and offer our names. She seems distracted, but soon seats us at a small table along the back walkway. This mistress-of-her-domain ushers patrons out of chairs with aplomb if they unknowingly seat themselves without putting their names on the list. It helps to be on a list,

unless you're the octopus that appears on the table adjacent. I don't think I could bear eating so close a cousin in the spectrum of sentience, so hunch over the indecipherable menu like a penitent. Find what I think is *shark*, and decide I can eat a fellow predator. It arrives in a bed of lettuce, spiced and tender, as befitting a carnivore. Linda has prawns—further down the food chain—and when all is eaten we feel oddly grateful, like supplicants at prayer. This body and blood of Spain. Finally,

the afternoon heat becomes unbearable, and we hop-scotch the shaded streets back to our cool flat for another sacrament: a *siesta* nap. Till night wakes Sevilla from sleep, and we swim her balmy streets.

> *The shark reincarnates*
> *in my body*

Interlude: Portugal & Spain as Fraternal Twins

Somewhat randomly, I look on the web for commentary about the differences between Portuguese and Spanish cultures. We've experienced both, but not long enough to tease-out the nuances. There are many stories to be had, from outsiders and insiders alike. Like any family. We'll start with Iain:

> I lived in Lisbon for 8 months and have spent a year in various parts of Spain. On the surface the two are very similar. They have bullfighting, wine production, romance language, similar architecture, both had massive new world empires and eventually became fascist states.
>
> I would say the Portuguese are more patriotic. The Spanish have their internal divisions and relate strongly to their autonomous communities just as much as being Spanish.
>
> The Spanish are much more supportive of you learning their language. The Portuguese almost seemed offended that you had an accent or couldn't speak it perfectly after a few months.
>
> I found it amusing that it's not illegal to smoke at a petrol station in Portugal.
>
> Sometimes the Portuguese seem very melancholic. They have a word for it; saudade. It's basically melancholic nostalgia, but not necessarily for something you've experienced yourself.
>
> I find the Spanish to be a bit loud, they really don't have volume control, annoying at night but fun and interesting...
>
> From the outside I perceive them to be more similar than different. If you express that to a Portuguese person do it tactfully, they are fiercely non-Spanish.

And there's this, from Gari:

> I have lived in Spain and have visited Portugal. In general, Portugal seems to do all it can to not 'be' Spanish. Spain finds it relatively easy not to be Portuguese. Some differences are: Portugal embraces British media more than Spain. Foreign TV is subtitled in Portugal and dubbed in Spain; as a result, Portuguese tend to speak English better.
>
> Spain tends to see itself as the bigger brother to Portugal and to some extent Portugal is both pissed off and accepting of this. Portugal is more outward-looking (it has a history of being Europe's explorers). Spain tends to be more

focused on its own success in comparison to Portugal, who are not so nation-centric.

Having said that: Both countries are changing. Spain's suffering from the 2008 financial crisis has [revealed] its vulnerability. Portugal is becoming a tourist destination to rival that of Spain.

These are "outsider" views from itinerant travelers, but straight-forward and practical. Here's something a bit more historical, from Rogelio, a Spaniard:

First, I think the Portuguese and Spanish societies are as close to each other (or more in some aspects) as the Scandinavian countries. There are more differences within Spain between, say, a Castilian and an Andalusian or Catalan than between a (Spanish) Galician and a Portuguese, and overall Spaniards and Portuguese clearly see themselves far closer to each other than to the French or the British.

However, if we want to highlight the differences, I will add the following: No, there is no siesta. Unless you're unemployed, retired, on vacation or live in a small village, there's just no opportunity for siesta in modern Spanish society. In fact, Spaniards, with the Portuguese and Greek, work some of the longest (not necessarily most productive) hours in Europe. In the meantime we just overdose with coffee to get by.

There's far more regional variation in Spain than in Portugal. It's not just that there are several languages in use, there are major differences even among the Spanish speakers. For example, I am from Madrid but my ancestors come from the northern regions of Leon and Soria, and I would rather be dead than caught dancing Flamenco.

Portugal as a whole has more cultural ties with the sea than Spain. Yes, Spain has a longer coast and has historically been a seafaring nation, but there are vast regions in the interior that have no cultural ties with the sea. Up until the end of the 20th century it was not unusual to find Spaniards that hadn't seen the sea in their entire lives.

Spain is more removed from its colonial past than Portugal. While both Spain and Portugal retained African colonies until the 1970's, the Spanish possessions of Equatorial Guinea, Morocco and the Western Sahara were relatively small and late additions which were never colonized to the extent that the centuries-old Portuguese colonies in Angola and Mozambique were.

When these colonies finally gained independence, life in Spain was largely unaffected. Portugal on the other side engaged in multiple military conflicts

> that were one of the triggers of the Carnation Revolution that brought democracy to the country, and received a massive influx of immigration (around a million people for a country that had barely 9 million inhabitants at the time).

After reading this discussion online, Jose—a Portuguese doctor—chimes in:

> Besides what others have already said, you can see the main differences between the Spanish and Portuguese way of living (and acting) by:
>
> 1. seeing what happens in major cities in both countries after 7 pm:
>
> —in Spain, you'll see lots of people gathering outdoors near tapas' bars with their relatives, including children and even babies, socializing, speaking loud, drinking and amusing themselves
>
> —in Portugal, you'll notice that most people just go home for dinner (or maybe to the supermarket to buy last minute ingredients to cook for dinner)
>
> 2. listening to their typical music. The Spanish Flamenco is a vibrant kind of music, while the typical Portuguese Fado is a sad, melancholic rhythm.
>
> Maybe this is an oversimplification, but I hope it helps.

This, as much as any historical tome or museum abstract, is what I wanted. Just people talking.

> *Now, stories fly*
> *fast as light*

Waking slow in Sevilla. Dreams I can't quite remember. Before entering the fray on this our last day, I read, hear the cathedral bell strike once at 9:15am. Lorca says, in "Schoolboy's Song":

> *Light doesn't know what it wants.*
> *At its opaline edge*
> *it meets up with itself*
> *and returns.*

This, the entire matter, perhaps the whole reason for everything: light not knowing what it wants, becoming us to find out.

> *Spirit—a tourist*
> *wandering*
> *Earth*

Barcelona

The ninety-minute flight from Seville to Barcelona, while brief, entailed seven full hours of missed Uber rides, navigating airports, waiting on the tarmac, and finally, the grumpy taxi depositing us on a dark Barcelona street with towering 1950s apartment complexes, graffiti scrawled on the metal pull-down garage doors. The occasional young couple strolling about holding hands. We think it's kind of a millennial vacation haunt, and all will look better in the morning light. The problem

with being a writer is always looking for a room with a view. And come morning, we discover that while our top floor flat should have a view of grand Barcelona, especially from our adobe patio long as a bowling alley—it doesn't. The six-foot high walls provide privacy, certainly, but I have to stand on a chair to see over. And there it is, a city full of mystery, waiting. Meanwhile,

the sun already bullies us inside because there are no umbrellas, and no shade, anywhere. The apartment itself is as spare as a business man might want—nothing soft, no place to sit. Though it becomes fun to complain, eventually, tease the story into absurd depravations. Unlike

true pilgrims of old, who'd welcome storm, starvation, even flagellate themselves for good measure. Hoping for a good review.

God: endless rooms,
endless views

BARCELONA HAS TWO ARTISTS WOVEN INSIDE ITS HISTORY: Gaudi, and Picasso. As patrons of this city, we want to get to know them. So our first morning, we walk up the long urban hill to Gaudi's *Park Guell*, whose modernist-eye filled spaces with bizarre color and shape, like a Spanish Dr. Seuss of childhood lore. Gaudi loved Indian, Persian, and Japanese artistry—filling Barcelona with buildings built entire from the Collective Unconscious. The sound of names like bird wings.

> *Parc Güell (Catalan: Parc Güell ['parg 'gweʎ]; Spanish: Parque Güell), which began as Gaudi's home and was to become a creative residential community, is now a park composed of gardens and architectural elements located on Carmel Hill, in Barcelona, Catalonia, Spain.*

In Gaudi's bio is a glimpse of his artistic temperament:

> *Gaudí observed of Islamic art its spatial uncertainty, its concept of structures with limitless space; its feeling of sequence, fragmented with holes and partitions, which create a divide without disrupting the feeling of open space by enclosing it with barriers.*

The grounds are large, filled with ascending gardens and paths, guitarists in shaded nooks playing Spanish music. I am especially entranced by a threesome named Tablao Sur, who play "flamenco global fusion" and whose lead musician—poetic dark beard and eyes—springs into flamenco-inspired dance over and again. We're all

busking, one way or another. Offering what music we can in the smattering of years we have. A basilica, a painting, a city—the empty spaces themselves.

> *Gaudi gazes at Barcelona—*
> *stone seduced by*
> *color*

From hillside views in Parc Güell one can see Gaudí's immense Sagrada Família basilica in the distance. The city, so filled with his work that he is nearly synonymous with Barcelona itself. The modest but artful house he lived in has been turned into a small museum in the park, and there's a video-loop of his fascinating life.

> Antoni Gaudí i Cornet was a Catalan architect from Spain known as the greatest exponent of Catalan Modernism. Gaudí's works have a highly individualized, sui generis style. Most are located in Barcelona, including his main work, the church of the Sagrada Família.
>
> Gaudí's work was influenced by his passions in life: architecture, nature, and religion. His work transcended mainstream Modernisme, culminating in an organic style inspired by natural forms. His masterpiece, the still-incomplete Sagrada Família basilica, is the most-visited monument in Spain—earning him the nickname "God's Architect."
>
> Gaudí's quest for a new architectural language drew inspiration from visits to the mountain of Montserrat, the caves of Mallorca, the saltpetre caves in Collbató, the crag of Fra Guerau in the Prades Mountains behind Reus, the Pareis mountain in the north of Mallorca and Sant Miquel del Fai in Bigues i Riells. All the while, looking to Nature for the secrets of design.

To see one artist's vision writ large as a city is, well, overwhelming—and worth every euro of the entry fee. After, famished and thirsty, we walk back down the hill, stop at a sweet courtyard for veggie burgers and fries at Café Flanders. Under the shade of trees, we reflect on the different feel of Barcelona from Sevilla, Lisbon, and Porto—more of a vast urban space we're still getting used to. Then, a bit of grocery shopping before heading back to our strange apartment with no view. At night,

I stand on tip-toe to peer over the patio walls and recognize, now, the lit Sagrada Família basilica rung with lights—still being built toward God. The dark scaffolding bearing the weight of the human best it can.

> *Gaudi asks God,*
> *again, for a new*
> *color*

OUR SECOND MORNING IN BARCELONA. WE WALK to the enchanting Placa de John Lennon (Lennon's Square) for late morning cappuccino and chocolate croissant. Linda has orange juice and sits on a far bench to write while watching the plaza's activity. I read *The Last Great Cause*, marvel at stories of writers caught in the vision and madness of the Spanish civil war. Across the square, the Beatles still walk through their Abbey Road album cover painted large on the side of a building. How Lennon became memorialized in this square is the morning's Zen *koan*,

as is the young woman who sits down at a table adjacent, talks loudly into her cell on speaker-phone so the plaza can hear everything. Luckily, it's in Spanish so I can't understand a word. Nearby, a very old woman reminds me of my mother before she died, moves slowly from walker to bench. Each move deliberate and pained. I notice how she and the young woman look similar in a strange way. Eerie. While children run to recess from a school bordering the plaza, play against the backdrop of John Lennon's stenciled face on a wall opposite. Saying, *Imagine...*

> *The Last Great Cause–*
> *this very moment*

Gaudí's Sagrada Família basilica exceeds my wilder hopes, looming sudden along the avenues like a gargantuan dinosaur or mountain or space-cathedral. Stone sculptures and mosaics warp the walls with mythological and invented figures as though Jung, Freud, Jehovah and Dr. Suess conspired to reveal divine and demonic figures in passion play. For Gaudí, the organic mycelial rooting and flowering of life itself grows from dirt to sky like weighty praise. Luminous stained-glass lighting the kaleidoscopic spaces. Stunned, we swarm this spirit-hive like tiny ants looking for wings.

HISTORY OF THE BASÍLICA

The Sagrada Família is a one-of-a-kind temple. Fruit of the genius architect Antoni Gaudí, the project was promoted by the people for the people. Five generations now have watched the Temple progress in Barcelona. Today, more than 140 years after the laying of the cornerstone, the Basilica continues to be built.

The Sagrada Família's construction was interrupted by the Spanish Civil War. In July 1936, revolutionaries set fire to the crypt and broke their way into the workshop, partially destroying Gaudí's original plans, drawings and plaster models, which led to 16 years of work to piece together the fragments of the master model. Construction resumed in the 1950s. However, some of the project's greatest challenges remain, including the construction of ten more spires, each symbolizing an important spiritual figure.

Late in life, Gaudí moved from his house in Parc Güell to a workshop in the basilica itself, living inside his masterpiece till he died in a tram accident at 73 years of age. Looking like a tramp, no one realized for days it was the great Gaudí till someone recognized him in the hospital. Unperturbed, he'd laid plans for the work to continue. I thought I saw his face under the gleaming yellow umbrella-parachute keeping the crucified Christ aloft in the high eaves. The face of Jesus like Gaudí's,

like anyone's caught between ascent and descent, wondering which way the spirit will move today. If militias will set fire to this cathedral of a world, or if we'll piece together the original plan, fragment by fragment, one impossible dream at a time.

The golden parachute is rung
with lights, the stone floor
with gravitas

Wandering old town Barcelona, we spy the Museu Picasso de Barcelona near the Mediterranean Sea. I pose, happy to be the least famous man. The museum is a unique repository of Picasso's early work, notes, sketches, and paintings. Born in Malaga, Andalucía, Pablo spent several years of his youth in Barcelona and studied at the prestigious art academy La Llotja, where his father was a professor. Picasso met many artists, and his first exhibitions took place in the artists' café Els Quatre Gats and the gallery Sala Parès. He was intimate with Barcelona throughout his life, which I had not known.

I am drawn to a room of b&w photos, Picasso enjoying his favorite pastime as he got older: listening to music played by friends, eating, talking long into the night. It was on one of these treasured evenings that Picasso finally passed away from heart failure at age 91. What one might call a good death. When a body becomes a city, an oeuvre of color and fragments that we fashion into a man.

When the music stops,
the body becomes
transparent

In Barcelona, one cannot be true to the city without sitting in a café and waxing philosophical. Or at least gossiping. History is a kind of gossip, so in John Lennon Square I read of Picasso and the Spanish Civil War. Remember that a life is imbedded in particulars of culture and era that irrevocably shape it. There is no art without it.

> At the start of the Spanish Civil War in 1936, Picasso was 54 years of age. Soon after hostilities began, the Republicans appointed him "director of the Prado, albeit in absentia," and "he took his duties very seriously," according to John Richardson, supplying the funds to evacuate the museum's collection to Geneva. The war provided the impetus for Picasso's first overtly political work. He expressed anger at Francisco Franco and fascists in The Dream and Lie of Franco (1937), which was produced "specifically for propagandistic and fundraising purposes." This surreal fusion of words and images was intended to be sold as a series of postcards to raise funds for the Spanish Republican cause.
>
> In 1944, Picasso joined the French Communist Party. He attended the 1948 World Congress of Intellectuals in Defense of Peace in Poland, and in 1950 received the Stalin Peace Prize from the Soviet government. Party criticism in 1953 of his portrait of Stalin as insufficiently realistic cooled Picassos interest in Soviet politics, though he remained a loyal member of the Communist Party until his death. His dealer, D-H. Kahnweiler, a socialist, termed Picasso's communism "sentimental" rather than political, saying "He has never read a line of Karl Marx, nor of Engels of course." In a 1945 interview with Jerome Seckler, Picasso stated: "I am a Communist and my painting is Communist painting. ... But if I were a shoemaker, Royalist or Communist or anything else, I would not necessarily hammer my shoes in a special way to show my politics." His commitment to communism, common among continental intellectuals and artists at the time, has long been the subject of some controversy; a notable demonstration thereof was a quote by Salvador Dalí (with whom Picasso had a rather strained relationship):
>
> "Picasso is a painter, so am I; [...] Picasso is a Spaniard, so am I; Picasso is a communist, neither am I."

As a pilgrim, masquerading as a tourist (or is it the other way around), I sip my coffee in John Lennon Square and imagine. How in his shoes, marinated in his beloved countries of Andalusia and France, faced with Franco and Hitler, I might have become as inevitable. Or Pablo, in my shoes, may have come to Spain as a California boy from a small town to gawk, lean into Barcelona like an old friend.

> *Gossip—the decades*
> *tell their*
> *stories*

THE FRENCH COUNTRYSIDE

THE TRAIN FROM NANTES, FRANCE EVENTUALLY BRINGS US to Port-Boulet where we are met by Mark, an English ex-pat who with his wife Debbie live in central France, run a small biking business called Loire Valley Breaks. He drives us to the nearby village of Bourgueil where we stay in the lovely old stone farmhouse Le Cour, hosted by a gentleman named Dominique.

Nothing much happens in Bourgueil, unless you're a local. Family and gossip and the weekly market fill the days year upon year. Bourgueil's population has remained four thousand souls since the 1700s. Mark—who is quite the talker—has honed his French accent for decades but to no avail. The villagers—kindly and humorously—note every error of this Brit's tongue; and ours, well, we might as well be from Mars.

We are here, though, not for language (though it is beautiful) but for a week of biking the French countryside. The Loire Valley ripe with green and river and sunflower, old off-road paths past decaying crucifixes, stone buildings at lonely crossroads, the occasional chateau or castle. Here, history has ground to a halt—and the only political agenda seems peace. *Could I live in a world without war*, the thought comes as my wife plays peek-a-boo off-road in a field of sunflowers stretching farther than the eye can see.

Without war, the castles
would be lonely

BIKING THE FRENCH COUNTRYSIDE, WE ARE ENTRANCED by mile after mile of trails through fields of sunflowers. As idyllic as one can imagine, and Linda loves sunflowers! Oddly enough,

as in Morocco, here they are grown mainly for their seeds. The astonishing beauty of fields of yellow an aesthetic by-product. For the artist, the beauty itself is the grail of color and madness. Enough to cut off an ear for. Or, like the cornfield in *Field of Dreams*, to disappear inside of.

Like a bee,
I bathe in gold

IN THE FRENCH COUNTRYSIDE, I FIND LITTLE MOTIVATION TO WRITE. The bike replaces the pen, the green fields reveal what blank paper can never be. Lollygagging in a meadow by the river. The flat trails and small hills, legs like wings. Even the occasional castle loses its luster. I could almost ride like this forever. Almost.

> *Blue sky, brown trail,*
> *green heart—desire*
> *less*

Our last day of biking the Loire Valley. We rise early so Mark can take us to the medieval town of Chinon, where the famous French writer Francois Rabelais was born. Despite endless sunflowers and green meadows, a book sometimes calls. France does love its writers, and Rabelais plaques and statues are prominent here in Chinon. To understand something of France, Mark says, is to visit for a spell with Francois.

François Rabelais was a French Renaissance writer, physician, humanist, monk and Greek scholar—primarily known as a writer of satire, of the grotesque, and of bawdy jokes and songs. Ecclesiastical and anticlerical, Christian and considered by some a free thinker, a doctor, a "bon vivant," the multiple facets of his personality sometimes seem contradictory. Caught up in the religious and political turmoil of the Reformation, Rabelais showed himself to be both sensitive and critical towards the great questions of his time.

Admirer of Erasmus, handling parody and satire, Rabelais fights for tolerance, peace, an evangelical faith and the return to the knowledge of ancient Greco-Roman, beyond the "Gothic darkness" that characterizes the Middle Ages.

As we leave the Château de Chinon that houses much of the city's history, Rabelais again waits for us by the river. As though keeping watch on the gothic darkness of our current obsessions. Perhaps he'd have been the worst kind of internet social influencer, or the best, or both. He sits with his back to the river, staring at the viewer, unperturbed. Evangelical in his humanism and humor. Waiting for us, it seems, to get the joke of any manifesto that takes itself too seriously.

A bird flies, craps
on the great writer's
head

Italy in Summer

A LONG TRAVEL DAY BRINGS US TO ISABELLA'S FLAT in Torino. Turin, on the English maps, but Torino here in Italy. Just as Seville, in Spain, is really Sevilla. We are met by Philippe, who is curating his mother's old apartment, a book-lover who died last year from Covid. Philippe lives upstairs, so is available to help navigate the flat with hand gestures and a bit of English. It's a funky, colorful set of rooms on the second floor of a residential neighborhood two blocks from the Po River—the longest river in Italy which flows eastward from the Alps. Spacious, stocked with old books and art, a marvelous kitchen of immense windows letting in light, and the aura, still, of the Italian mother who lived here for years. At a bargain price, too, since we're the first tenants since her death. I suspect we'll get to know Isabella during our two-week sojourn: a delightful haunting.

The sun peeks inside
at Isabella's new
friends

THE HEAT WAVE IN EUROPE IS CATCHING UP WITH US, but we still want to give Turino a go. The Po River here is wide but marshy, with only a little flow. But we can see the mountains in the distance where the river begins, purple against the sunset afterglow. The streets teem with locals and tourists eating dinner in the restaurants that line the avenues. Early morning and evenings are civilized, while the heat of the day chases you from shadow to shadow. If Apocalypse comes,

will we simply eat later, wander the avenues by moonlight, light candles till early morning, when the solar dragon opens its eye, breaths?

> *Air-conditioning–*
> *the ark we*
> *enter*

SITTING IN ISABELLA'S FLAT EARLY MORNING, WINDOWS FLUNG wide, I scan the news as the heat begins to rise. This report from countries we've just visited catches my eye:

> PARIS/LISBON, July 16 (Reuters) Wildfires raged in southwestern France and Spain on Saturday, forcing thousands of people to be evacuated from their homes as blistering summer temperatures put authorities on alert in parts of Europe...
>
> In the latest weather warning, 38 of France's 96 departments were listed on "orange" alert, with residents of those areas urged to be vigilant.
>
> MOROCCO BLAZES
> Across the Mediterranean from Europe, blazes in Morocco ripped through more than 2,000 hectares of forest in the northern areas of Larache, Ouazzane, Taza and Tetouane, killing at least one person, local authorities said. More than 1,000 households were evacuated from their villages and water-carrying planes helped extinguish most of the fires by Friday night.

Sounds like the California we left two months ago. Eerie, to have just been in Portugal, Spain, Morocco, and France where the new fires have now erupted. As though Prometheus was fleeing what we stole from the gods: knowledge, unheeded. Burning the house of Earth down.

> *The shade invites*
> *like a ruined*
> *lover*

[Prometheus is best known for defying the Olympian gods by stealing fire and giving it to humanity in the form of technology, knowledge, and more generally, civilization. In some versions of the myth, he is also credited with the creation of humanity from clay.]

I MAY STICK WITH TURIN BECAUSE THE ITALIAN TORINO reminds me too much of that American speedster, the Ford Gran Torino. And, of course, the Clint Eastwood film called *Gran Torino*, so think I'll stay with Turin for now. It is still humid and hot—

I find Linda happily ensconced on the small outdoor balcony, moving just inside the open doors of the living room when the rain comes. She loves rain. She looks happy. I leave her to her silences as drops begin splashing through the open kitchen windows; I reluctantly close them till the downpour is spent, mop the window-sill with towels. Then re-open the flat to the fierce faces of dark storm clouds. This grand moment—perhaps it's why we came all this way: to sit for a spell in Isabella's old kitchen. To escape the speed, the bluster of America.

The thunder roars,
the lightning
follows

silver angels collide
between sky
& earth

Isabella's apartment. I sit adjacent the floor-to-ceiling bookshelf filled with her books, smatterings of ceramics, butterflies in glass, a candle, a large silver serving-chalice, memorabilia. It's an odd experience: so many books at my fingertips, yet I am unable to read most because of their Italian script. But like a child, I can look at the pictures, guess from the titles what she was interested in before dying last year of Covid. Travel books—Istanbul, the tropics, Japan, the Italian coastline. A book about the galaxy beyond our solar system. Art books—Klimt, Alberti, Baroque architecture, Moroccan interiors, and the art of gardens. Isabella seems to have loved gardens.

There *is* one book in English, *The Illustrated Virago Book of Women Travellers.* I open to a page about Maud Parrish (1878-1976) who, in her sole memoir entitled "Nine Pounds of Luggage," writes:

> "So I ran away. I hurried more than if lions had chased me. Without telling him. Without telling my mother or father. There wasn't any liberty in San Francisco for ordinary women. But I found some..."

> In her memoir, Maud Parrish relates her life of madcap adventure with the breathless, excitable energy of one who cannot stand still. Parrish worked as a dance-hall girl in Dawson City, Yukon, and Nome, Alaska (after she had fled from an ill-fated marriage), and operated a gambling house in Peking at the turn of the century. With her 'nine pounds of luggage' and a banjo, she claimed to have gone around the world sixteen times, up and down continents, around and about exotic islands. Parrish died at the age of ninety-eight.

I wonder: is this a glimpse into Isabella's dream, whose colorful flat we are enjoying? I like the mystery of this. Our pilgrimage here, Isabella's life in Italy—lingering together between the walls of this, her unwritten memoir.

Each ordinary life—
its own wonder

In the early evening, Linda and I finally go out for a stroll. It is still 90-degrees, but we enjoy the exertion walking uphill to the nearby Chiesa di Santa Maria del Monte dei Cappuccini, an "iconic 16th century church on a hill with scenic views of the Po River, Torino, and sunsets." The church is a bit ragged on the outside, but who wouldn't be after seven centuries? We briefly sit inside while a mass is conducted—one of our strangely favorite things to do as unbelievers. The soaring stone, the soaring song, the glass stained with color, with the infinite longing of centuries.

The old priest seduces
my ear with
Latin

untranslatable
as a stream

THIS PILGRIMAGE TO OLD ANDALUSIA LEAVES ME WITH A BONE to chew. How now to spend the rest of my sixties, and if lucky, my seventies before the world becomes too hot to handle? Or my body, too old to care? Perhaps more of everything: helping to inch the world toward sanity by the butterfly effect of my own tiny wings. And if the world does go to hell in a hand-basket, then to nurture each other through whatever Last Days become the First Days of the new earth.

I just had to look up, *Going to hell in a hand-basket*. Who knew....

> In the 19th century, the phrase was associated with the American gold rush of the 1840s where men were lowered by hand in baskets down mining shafts to set explosives, which could have deadly consequences.

I'd prefer, of course, to use a hand-basket for picking wild berries, bringing hot soup to those in need. This, the destination of pilgrimage—to nurture *home* like there's no tomorrow.

> *Small wings flap here,*
> *storms gather*
> *there*
>
> *Earth—a mother*
> *adjusting her*
> *skirt*

In the Turin evening, we leave the flat for a long walk across the Po bridge. Meander down a stone quay used, in the past, for transport and sales. Now, there's one or two lonely cafes along the slow-moving river, haunted by graffiti-filled stone walls and metal doors boarded up. But as anthropologists of the Anthropocene, it is intriguing nonetheless.

We find a park that hugs the river, filled with young people in the hot evening: gymnasts balancing on ropes tied between trees; playing guitar, soccer, and a large beer-gaggle spilling onto the brown grass from a riverside bar. This section of the Po is deeper, allowing rowers practice-time in crews of four or two, with a few wandering kayaks going nowhere in particular. We enjoy the walk immensely—

but can't escape the heat wave gripping Europe, the smell of fire in the air, the drought that here has turned the wide lawns of the park brown. Everything with a brittle texture to it. But Turin has seen worse, and better, and in that laconic Italian tradition is a kind of eternity all its own. So,

we visit the gelato shop again—marvelous. Makes me feel like I'm on vacation, even in the End Times.

> *Chocolate and raspberry ice*
> *melt faster in this*
> *heat*

I FIND MYSELF DRAWN AGAIN TO THE BOOK IN ISABELLA'S FLAT I've left on the kitchen table for viewing: *The Illustrated Virago Book of Women Travellers*. It must have had special meaning for Isabella, whose shelves are filled with books of places like Morocco, Jordan, Martha's Vineyard, Rome, Turkey, and more. What strikes me is not only the remarkable adventures by these women who broke from the societal mores each inhabited in their time period, but that the tone of the writing, as the collection notes, is always personal. The male mind

of the day reported only the facts of travel, as though its main purposes lay in journalistic or scientific accounting (unless you were Rilke or Shelley or any of the suspect poets). My own style of travel-journaling is rooted in this feminine mind (archetypally), the *anima* perhaps of my own maleness. Or some such Jungian rubbish. Mainly,

I like sitting in Isabella's kitchen, the intimate world at our fingertips.

The table—set with tea
and world

AT ISABELLA'S TABLE AGAIN with *The Illustrated Virago Book of Women Travellers*. The editor Mary Morris—a professor at St. Lawrence College, whose memoir *All The Way to the Tigers* is blurbed by Oprah—mentions a divergence in the male and female mind when it comes to travel:

> As I read through the literature of male travel writers in the 1980s, I found that their experiences did not correspond to or validate my own. Most explored a world that is essentially external and revealed only glimpses of who and what they are, whom they long for, whom they miss. The writers' own inner workings in most cases (with marvelous exceptions such as Peter Matthiessen in The Snow Leopard, Henry Miller in The Colossus of Maroussi, and Colin Thubron in his travel books on China and Russia) are obscured.

She develops this theme in more detail, citing Lawrence Durrell's description of Freya Stark:

> "A great traveller is a kind of introspective as she covers the ground outwardly, so she advances inwardly."

> And indeed, for many women the inner landscape is as important as the outer, the beholder as significant as the beheld. The landscape is shaped by the consciousness of the person who crosses it. There is a dialogue between what is happening within and without.

As a man, maybe it is the woman in me that writes, and travels. At the end of the book's Introduction, Mary Morris muses that for those whose fate seems mired...

> If we grow weary of waiting, we can go on a journey. We can be the stranger who comes to town.

> > Isabella grew weary
> > of waiting and
> > left

AT A CAFÉ IN TURIN, I ENTERTAIN THE NEWS FOR A MOMENT, like a rogue set on ruining the pastoral Italian landscape. The far-right is on the rise again in the heart of Europe. America, of course, is not alone in this. We're not that far from book-burnings and inquisitions. I read a quote about opposing worries of George Orwell and Aldous Huxley that seems relevant these days.

> What Orwell feared were those who would ban books. What Huxley feared was that there would be no reason to ban a book, for there would be no one who wanted to read one. Orwell feared those who would deprive us of information. Huxley feared those who would give us so much that we would be reduced to passivity and egoism. Orwell feared that the truth would be concealed from us. Huxley feared the truth would be drowned in a sea of irrelevance. Orwell feared we would become a captive culture. Huxley feared we would become a trivial culture. In 1984, Huxley added, "people are controlled by inflicting pain. In Brave New World, they are controlled by inflicting pleasure. In short, Orwell feared that what we hate will ruin us. Huxley feared that what we love will ruin us."
>
> —Neil Postman

This elephant in the room, whatever end one peers at, is like the one I read in Kay Ryan's poem. They all sit beside me in this café, debating if there's room at the table:

THE ELEPHANT IN THE ROOM

The room is
almost all
elephant.
Almost none
of it isn't.
Pretty much
solid elephant.
So there's no
room to talk
about it.

The elephant suddenly glad to be the center of attention, and almost the size of a blank *haiku*:

I arrive at the Museo Nazionale del Risorgimento Italiano, a Turin history museum just a twenty minute walk from our flat. The initial exhibits are old and stuffy, with no air-conditioning, and most of it is (of course) in Italian. But the displays empty into a vast ballroom with immense paintings and statues worth the visit. Almost all of it about war. All of it, interesting—

famous and anonymous citizens, generation after generation, moving towards democratic rights and having a voice. Roaming Europe so freely these days, I feel the progress easily taken for granted now. It all depends

on the angle of light and shadow. In the vast ballroom of Italian wars and revolutions, the cavernous distance makes it seem palatable, even noble. But just north of here, the citizens of Kiev are under no such illusion. And south, the great fulcrum round Jerusalem never ceases its allure and apocalypse. Today, though, watching children spill from the exits,

I practice peace. There may be endless tyrants on the horizon, waiting to be painted in glory in the vacuous spaces of history. Where for a few *euros, dollars, rubles, shekels* we can admire the latest dead Caesar. Then forget them.

> *Laughing children in need*
> *of no translation*
> *no manifesto*

I WANDER THE GALLERINA SUBALPINA, AN ANTIQUE ARCADE with an array of shops and cafes, old and new. Find a tiny bookstore, La Casa del Libro Millenovecentoventisei which I peruse with reverence—assisted by the shopkeeper who says this book-enclave was established in 1926. She directs me to two small shelves of English language titles, and against hope, I indulge my passion and find one very old book to buy. It's wrapped now in an elegant package, which I'll unbind when I get home. Some mysteries are better kept under wrap.

> *The Universe is*
> *a green book waiting*
> *to be fathomed*

IN TURIN'S HEAT, I LAZE IN THE COOL OF ISABELLA'S FLAT, take a break from Italy's sordid and jubilant histories, read instead of snow. Peter Matthiessen's *The Snow Leopard,* where he traverses the Himalayas looking for signs. He quotes Lao Tzu's *Tao Te Ching*:

Before heaven and earth
There was something nebulous
    silent isolated
    unchanging and alone
    eternal
    the Mother of All Things
I do not know its name
I call it Tao

Darkness there was, wrapped in yet more Darkness... That One Thing... was born through the power of heat...

Unlike Matthiessen, my parents found a real patch of land on the way to Yosemite my father named Shangri La. Built an array of hexagons in the dense forest to retire to. After his death, climate change robbed the hills of trees till all became tinder. This morning, in Italy, I receive a text message from the property's caretaker Heather,

who says her family is being evacuated from Shangri La due to the explosion of the Oak Fire. Similar towns with similar dreams in California have already burned, like the town of Paradise a few years before in the Sierra foothills north of us. The texts from Heather, and my brother Steven, come as they prepare for sleep, which find me across the globe as I simultaneously wake. It'll be a long night for them, and a long day for me, helpless in Turin.

Snow may never return
to Himalayan peaks—

fire laps the mountains
jubilant in
heat

NOT WANTING TO DWELL ON A FIRE WE CAN'T CONTROL on the other side of the globe, we launch into the sea of heat that is Turin. Cloud and breeze make it seem cooler, hopscotching from shade to shade helps. We walk to Mole Antonelliana whose spire rises clearly above the Turin skyline.

> An architectural landmark of the city of Turin, it was initially conceived as a synagogue, before bought by the Municipality of Turin and made into a monument to national unity. Completed in 1889 with a height of 167.5 meters, it was the tallest brick building in Europe at the time. The panoramic lift was inaugurated in 1961, during the celebrations for the centenary of the Italian Unification and was renovated in 1999. Today it allows visitors to ascend to the panoramic terrace and take in amazing views of the city and the surrounding Alps.

The glass-walled elevator takes us 85 meters in 59 seconds to the 360-degree Panoramic Terrace. A beautiful sea of red tile roofs and stone buildings stretch for miles. As we roam Turin after, the Mole Antonelliana spire keeps popping into view along the skyline and round random building-corners when we least expect it. Like history— insisting on itself from every angle.

> *The glass walls of*
> *the elevator are*
> *transparent*

Inside Turin's Mole Antonelliana is The Temple of Cinema where one can watch the glass elevator ascend from a door in the floor skyward, till it disappears through a portal in the vaulted ceiling above. Where we'd stood just before on the Panoramic Terrace with its 360-degree views. Quite the vision.

We were not prepared for how extraordinary the six-floor "cinema temple extravaganza" would be. You walk the perimeter from the lower floor along an ascending ramp, looking one way into the central film-courtyard where a movie montage continuously plays below, watched by patrons on lounge-couches spread across the floor; or, wall-side, ingenious displays celebrate all aspects of movie-making—from original Italian silent films, to modern movies. There's a 3-D demonstration where you affix goggles to your head,

step inside 360-degree virtual worlds of a volcano, an astronaut training center, dinosaurs on the loose, and more. Further up the ramp are surreal displays where one can enter a large refrigerator, sit on faux-toilets to watch film clips. Leave it to the Italians. After a long spell, the line between the surreal and the real blurs. Like our modern moment—though there's no glass elevator to escape the kaleidoscopic chaos below. But who'd want to? "There's no better show on earth," The Temple of Cinema seems to say.

> *The crowd claps even when*
> *monsters appear*

The whole world feels afire. Yet I am desperate to wander Turin despite the 96-degree heat that, with humidity, feels like 106-degrees. Walk the now-familiar Po Avenue to the Palazzo Madama, a palace, art and history museum. The twenty-first century itself will one day, if we're lucky, occupy exhibits in museums like this. Makes me even more obsessed with eras already past since we, like them, are living history.

> *The Palazzo Madama embraces the entire history of the city of Turin: created as a Roman gate, it became a fortress in the Middle Ages and subsequently the castle of the Princes of Acaia. Between the Seventeenth and Eighteenth centuries it was selected as the residence of the royal dowagers of the Savoy family and, in the Nineteenth century, King Charles Albert chose it as the seat of the first Senate of the Kingdom of Italy. Since 1934 the palace has housed the antique art collections of the Museo Civico.*

The base floor houses a Shroud of Turin display, with images of Christ's face in painting and other artwork. The transparent floor shows original Roman foundations, and as one ascends the stairways, new eras unfold. I find an entire room of ecclesiastical pulpits and benches carved with playful wooden figures that are by no means pious. Monkish imps and pompous hierophants secreted among the religious props. And before I leave, a room of evocative paintings with palettes of rich color surprise the viewer. A baby Christ looking like a surfer dude, nonchalant and so cool, as if he knew wave after wave of the coming centuries might demand a sense of humor. Or at least an open heart.

In his mother's arms,
a child is supremely
confidant

As we wake in Turin, California goes to sleep. It appears the Oak Fire has swept up Wild Dove Lane in Mariposa and taken Shangri La. Clint, the last hold-out on the hill below Footman Ridge, said he had no choice but to evacuate. We spend the day facing the unthinkable, that my parents' beloved forest home is no more. It is surreal. Heather and family, who cared for the *wabi-sabi* property, were in another town shopping for groceries when the fire hit. Lost everything except the clothes on their back and the car they were driving. They're in shock. We're in shock. All of us worlds away from the paradise we've worked so hard to build.

> *On the fire map*
> *the red spreads*
> *everywhere*

In Turin, we wake to another day of the reality of fire halfway round the world: my parents' Shangri La disappearing into smoke. Surreal text exchanges with family, neighbors, renters—as they go to sleep, we wake. The Oak Fire has burned everything. The gaggle of rustic hexagons as invisible now as their fabled namesake. Stunned, we go ahead with our planned bike trip along the Po River—unable to bear sitting around the flat thinking about ruin.

Curving from streambed into old neighborhoods, I find a fitting street sign, stop for a photo. Nietzsche would be amazed at the solace his name brings, marooned on a random Italian alley next to a chain-link fence. Remembering his now-cliqued phrase, "That which does not kill us makes us stronger." As well as "Without music, life would be a mistake..." from Twilight of the Idols. To be an idol on a street-sign is still a noble destiny, I muse as we continue biking along the shrinking Po River. Find myself humming old church songs my family would mischievously reprise while sitting in the Big Hex of our new age dreams. *Swing low, sweet chariot, comin' for to carry me home...* And whether it's Jesus or Nietzsche himself greeting me in the end, the wild ride is still worth every mortal minute.

> *Smoke, like mist*
> *embodies grief & mystery*
> *twinned*

FAR ALONG THE TURIN BIKE PATH, WE STOP FOR A LATE LUNCH at La Luna e i Falò, a beautiful local restaurant off a turn along the Po River.

A cool respite from the heat, amply filled with Italian locals, hosted by a warm and dignified older man who welcomes us and takes our orders. Pizza for me, ravioli for Linda, though I think we may have ordered something different than we thought. Ah, language and its vicissitudes! No matter. The restaurant's walls are filled with small murals of Italian sayings, lightening the smoky weight of California fire still blanketing our hearts. The most beautiful of powers, laughter makes the day bearable. Everyone in this restaurant, I'm sure, has known loss, grief, death in some way, or will. In Italy, I am reminded how big the heart can be, needs to be, in this furnace of a world.

Italian
Chi sa farti ridere ha il più bello dei poteri

English (US)
Who knows how to make you laugh has the most beautiful of powers

> *The waiter brings us food*
> *as though feeding*
> *the world*

The only way Heather, our caretaker in Shangri La, was able to take photos of the fire's aftermath is because of the "press pass" received from a local Fox News channel, allowing official access to document the Oak Fire. We view them while still in Turin: sobering and surreal.

Besides a few burnt trees, the only thing left standing is my mother's iconic glass meditation hex. Built with her own hands. What fire could not melt. All the other hexagons in our wistful village are gone. Or rather, reduced to piles of ash, mingled with shells of a water heater here, a sink there. Marooned in Italy to bear this mourning, I remember:

> *The First Hex*, where my parents first lived—a small studio built from a "kit," outpost on the edge of wilderness.
>
> *The Jade House*, another small hex with a gorgeous loft, where I lived for a short spell after graduate school, later becoming one of the prime B&B rentals for *Shangri La*.
>
> *Tea House I*, built as a semi-traditional Japanese sleeping room for guests.
>
> *Tea House II*, or *The Magic Hex*, which brother Scott paid for Dad to build after he won his first big magic award, with full ceiling to floor mirrors to practice close-up magic in.
>
> *The House of Serenity*, or *The Big Hex*, an astonishing feat of impromptu architecture by my parents, a wraparound kitchen arcing round the large interior space. The site of many a workshop, ritual celebration, Thanksgiving and Christmas dinner, sleepovers with grandkids on the wide floor, movies and popcorn and desserts.
>
> The tiny five-sided *Pentangle* where mother used to do stained-glass work, now completing its existence in ash.
>
> My father's rectangular *Workshop*, with all the old tools, and the new tools of our renters.

The Village of Shangri La is now ash and rubble. As someone said, the aftermath fits my father's other name for this vision, The Land of New Beginnings. Whether for rebuilding, or to lay fallow for a long spell as the brittle Sierra Nevada finds its balance again, with-or-without human beings.

> *Turin's heat a future-memory*
> *of what may already be*
> *lost*

IN CALIFORNIA AGAIN, I UNWRAP THE OLD BOOK from one of Turin's bookstores, the only book I bought in Europe. The cover is a faded green embossed hardback with a butterfly or moth etched on the cover at the top, and the title circling what seems to be an owl in flight. Inside:

THE UNIVERSE:
or,

THE INFINITELY GREAT
AND THE INFINITELY LITTLE

By
F. A. Pourchet, M.D.

Illustrated by 270 Engravings on Wood,

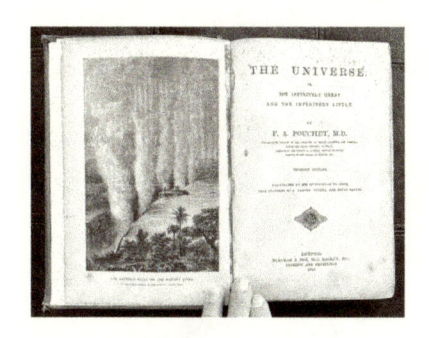

From Drawings by A. Faguet, Mesnel, and Emile Bayard. LONDON: Blackie & Son, Old Bailey, E.C.; Glasgow and Edinburgh. 1883.

I love old books, particularly from the 1800's or earlier with romantic notions of explaining the entire Universe from that era's vantage. It's a kind of Zen *koan*, this ephemeral nature of knowledge. The beauty, conceits, emerging truths and outrageous errors of science and speculation. The sum total boiled down into a modest tome filled with hieroglyphic squiggles of black lines and illustrations. This old book from a previous century, found on a Turin bookshelf among only two shelves of English-language books, has found its way to America, for a spell. This mini-universe of the infinitely great and the infinitely small. Unsure which size my country is now, or my own heart, or you, the reader?

> Like Alice in Wonderland—
> I shrink and grow
> scandalously

New England in Autumn

NEW YORK FLOODED THE DAY AFTER WE LEFT for the Hudson Valley by train. The big news of it on my little phone, subways filling with rainwater—I hadn't known we needed to escape. We'd spent four days walking Greenwich Village, seduced by jazz clubs, the Tenement Museum with its musty wood and vibrant immigrant stories. Then a misty Central Park with endless curving paths; the MET filled to the brim with ancient arts and modern abstractions. One world riffing into another, decaying, resurrecting. Falling in love with the whole enigma of us, again.

I'd last visited this megalopolis decades before, when an early poem about my young son appeared in the classic *Hudson Review*. After the reading, we'd gathered after in the infamous Chelsea Hotel where writers had lived and drank and smoked their way to anonymity and, if lucky, momentary stardom. Now,

we are both older, and the city is older, and the earth groans with more rain than New York can hold. The waters, spilling into tunnels like mercurial commuters. We escaped speeding north through valley and forest to Vermont for a week of biking through autumn color and sun-drenched meadows. This trip scheduled by luck and omen in-between New England's own floods. I wanted to see the brilliant hues of trees before they all get washed away. And the bicycle becomes, by necessity, a boat.

> *When my grandson is old*
> *he might read this and*
> *wonder*
>
> *The leaf was orange-yellow,*
> *the waters opaque*
> *blue*

On the bike trip through Vermont, our guide Alex says people think of it as the green state, with one cow for every six people. The Green Mountains verdant, church steeples nestled in the valleys. It certainly looks this way as we bike through winding hills. But in the early 1800's forests had been clear-cut for farming, and one day

George Marsh returned to his family farm in Woodstock shocked to find the hillsides of Mount Tom denuded of trees and soil eroding into streams. He knew that local families would soon be robbed of their livelihoods by survival instincts alone. Eventually, he penned *Man and Nature* proclaiming "humans need to be stewards of nature." His book prompted forestland management and, eventually, the state's environmental movement. Even the cows, now, generate electricity with their prolific manure, stored in anaerobic digesters that spin invisible power.

I find his book in Burlington at The Crow Bookshop, right alongside volumes of the original Abenaki peoples, who knew how to steward the land long before George.

> *The forests watch humans*
> *pass like wind*
> *or fire*

[Note: Forests were cleared not only for farming, but the creation of potash. Asheries cooked hardwood ashes with water to make a black substance pulling sand from glass to improve the firing of ceramics. Europe and North American desire for its use in homes and art created high demand, and the potash from an acre of hardwood helped poor settlers eke out a living in the rocky hills.]

BIKING THROUGH RED MAPLE TREES IN QUEBEC AND VERMONT, I remember the story. Indigenous Abenaki tapping trees to provide sugar in their diet. Boiling sap into granulated bits, hence the term *sugaring*. Passing this knowledge to colonists, who liked being able to make a living from the forest itself. We pass sugar shacks that started as simple lean-tos, gradually becoming more elaborate. In many towns they are still the center of spring social life, drawing distanced neighbors together. They say during the Civil War, people in the north turned to maple syrup to protest cane and corn sugar that relied on slave labor. We each have our stories.

At the end of the day's ride, an old Vermont farmer gives a talk during happy hour, says that proper tapping does no permanent damage to the tree. He knows of maple trees tapped for over a hundred years that are still alive and well! But as the hour winds down and the drinks find their bottom, he worries that a changing climate threatens the end of sugaring as a way of life. Says he'll keep tapping till the end.

> *The red maple has*
> *no idea of*
> *its own sweetness*

VERMONT IS SMALL. AMERICA IS BIG. The small sits inside what is big, but the big has trouble fitting amiably inside the small. Traveling modest country roads, we pass modest family farms, thousands tucked between hills and lakes. In most towns, there's a farmers market selling organic greens and meats, creamy goat cheese, tendered daily from Vermont fields. I stop to taste. All food should be so good. I ask one farmer why it can't be. She says it's the big things: rising fuel and feed costs. A fast food culture that favors corporate agriculture. Many farmers face the decision: condos or cows? New Englanders are fiercely independent, too; she winks, says "we need help thinking collectively."

Our cycle guides say that, ironically, small farms are disappearing while restaurants are proliferating. Many of the best chefs want to feature what is locally grown, but rarely have time to stop at each farm, chat with the owners and figure out when the Swiss chard or haricot vert will be ready for the following week. All it takes, though, are a few souls to travel between farms, link chefs and seasons, and the small takes on a bigger life than its own. Even the state—perhaps because it's small—is helping this organic network grow.

At one market, I ask for an apple. New England apples have 150 names—McIntosh, Delicious, Empire, Rome, Spartan, Cortland and Northern Spy just to name a few. You become, I suspect, what you love—spartan, an empire, a spy for the greater good.

> *One bite is enough*
> *to dream a small*
> *paradise*

OUR BIKING GUIDE ALEX HAS ANOTHER STORY. Vermonters learned to trust the land, he says, not unlike the Abenaki before them. Vermont had lost 90 percent of its farms. Famous for pastoral landscapes and small towns, losing this way of life was almost unthinkable. Yet the world kept changing: developers offering million-dollar buyouts, an improvement over genocide, but the land would still suffer.

"But even in America," Alex says as we ride side-by-side on the trail under color of autumn, "you can develop a land trust." Vermonters approached farmers, offered to buy development rights for their land so it could never be used for anything except farming. Thus preserving a way of life. "Condos and shopping malls would be here otherwise," this ex-tenured history professor from Oklahoma opined. And we ride in silence the rest of the way, under a canopy of leaves orange, brown, yellow, and red red red.

Ancestral grounds
never lose
their storytellers

At the tiny border-crossing between Vermont and Quebec, we stand in the modest queue for 20 minutes while the Canadian border guard becomes suspicious of the touring van carrying us bikers north. He wants to search each and every bag. For drugs? Because we're Americans? Worthy of suspicion now?

The guard settles for two random bag checks. Our biking guides have never encountered this before, and the American border guards, stopping traffic coming the other way into Vermont, are laughing, wondering what we've done to piss off the Canadians. More suspicious than the two burly French-bikers dressed in black on big motorcycles? Or the too-cute older Quebec couple riding between countries, returning home just a mile inside the border?

We're all suspicious, I suspect, to someone. Secretly, I long for inspection from head to toe. To stand naked at the border of you and me. To be worthy.

> *The guard lets us pass*
> *waving his hand*
> *like a king*

IN THE DIM LIGHT OF THE MONTREAL MUSEUM, I fall in love with the names of the First Peoples: Abenakis, Algonquins, Atikamekw, Cree, Huron-Wyandot, Maliseet, Mi'kmaqs, Iroquois, Innu and Naskapis. How they knew themselves in the time before words is forever lost. Still, if one remembers, a world, for a moment, is born from oblivion. I run my tongue over each vowel, the proud consonants, peer at old photos, drawings, the eyes looking back wondering which of us are the ghosts?

> *The land welcomes*
> *even her careless children*

We are driven to the Montreal airport by a broad-smiling man from Haiti, who came to America with family before settling in Quebec—his Haitian French helping to navigate this new land. At the airport, Linda and I are struck by how friendly the Canadian airport staff are. Faces, mostly black, accents mostly French, as though understanding the essential fragility of journeys.

As we pass to U.S. Customs, the American staff are dead-pan serious—some fundamental paranoia, perhaps, of boundaries, of what can happen. Linda is randomly tagged for a full backpack search of her belongings, a red stamp put on her boarding pass after (for unknown reason), causing new moments of delay. "A little old lady terrorist alert," we laughed after. At yet another checkpoint, Linda makes the mistake of answering "Yes" about having anything to declare: *an orange*, prompting a long wait for a supervisor to finally come and ask her about the orange, and that, yes, we'll have to leave it behind.

> *The orange—a language*
> *undeclared*

In Camden, Maine, sun streams through immense windows of this old stone library. Illuminating history one might blindly pass unaware. Like this column by a young woman in the free *Camden Herald*, hungry for lost stories

of indigenous peoples who lived here first: Penobscot and Passamaquoddy. And the muddy history of the region's European "founders" George Weymouth and Samuel Waldo who blithely kidnapped and killed the locals. She finds an 1883 editorial by Nathan C. Fletcher in the *Rockland Opinion*:

> The Indians in great numbers met Captain Weymouth and his company, when they landed upon our shores, in a friendly manner and brought their furs to exchange... and the Englishmen repay them by invading...wrenching from the mother's fond arms the best beloved boy, and from the father the girl, the delight of his eyes, who cheered him in his lonely hours... [These] children of nature, who roamed the Everglades of the Megunticook valley, and rested upon the crests of these mountains, upon which I am now gazing, are entitled to [be remembered]...

A newspaper, like smoke, is a tale: the murder of amnesia, or a fire to tell true stories by. A tourist may travel through landscapes and never once hear the absence, while a lost pilgrim listens, looks. This dark practice of history:

> *What we cannot see*
> *is simply*
> *everywhere*

IN THE CORNER TIBETAN STORE, I WATCH VISITING MONKS on the floor in the back room creating an intricate sand mandala. Here, in Maine. Four squat monks in orange and burgundy, huddled studiously over their colorful creation, tapping long brass implements funneling dyed-sand into place. A faint light blue pattern etched on white paper beneath guides their hands. Helping the world take shape.

Why do Tibetan monks seem happy so often, despite exile, immolation. They've come all the way from Dharamsala, India, to raise funds for their monastery. They know the mandala, at the end of the week, will be destroyed, offered as prayer. Is this tourism? Begging? A gift of time, of impermanence? How did I find myself here, how did they, how do you dear reader?

> *I have no idea of the shape I am*
> *taking, though colorful clues*
> *abound*

Wandering Maine's small towns, I find Stone Soup Books in Camden up a beaten staircase like a wizard's shop. Paul and Agnes Joy have run this used bookstore since the 1980's. A tall, bearded man with a love of story, he sits folded into a tiny chair behind the wooden counter. Beckons me browse to my heart's content. A dangerous invitation.

I do my usual hunting through overwrought shelves for treasures, look for old books small enough to carry across the continent, not too expensive. I find them. Poignant, surreal visions of what America was supposed to be, could still be, though the gap now seems impassable:

> *The National Ode–The Memorial Freedom Poem [Illustrated]* published on the 100th anniversary of America in 1876.
>
> *America Was Promises*, Archibald MacLeish, published in 1939.

The first, a poem of grand vision, the second a reckoning: *promises for whom?*

> *Who is the traveler in this journey*
> *Deciphers the revolving night: receives*
> *The signal from the light returning?*
>
> *America was promises to whom?*

Archibald says *Believe the promises are theirs who take them...*but the brutal irony is stark in contemporary light.

Paul and I discuss these things till he notices my third book, a small hardback novel by the psychedelic pioneer Aldous Huxley entitled *Antic Hay*, published in 1923. A spoof, apparently, on proper society—"antic hay" an "absurd dance" coined by Christopher Marlowe in the old play *Edward II*. Paul tells stories of Aldous living for a spell in Camden, exploring psilocybin with colleagues who came and went. Trying to make sense of an absurd world. A book or country, like a mushroom, a kind of dream? A fiction? A mad dance?

> *Each reader deciphering*
> *signals of lost light–fading?*
> *Returning?*

WE PULL INTO THE DIRT DRIVEWAY OF COBB HILL COHOUSING & Farm in Vermont, make our way up the hill to Sandy's house, the last in the row edged against meadow. We know her from another life in California before she retired here. And what a place! A tour of the farm reveals an active cheese-making business, machinating toilets that use only a cupful of sawdust. And a rambling communal house where folks gather for meals, workshops, play ping pong. A world all its own in the middle of America. Well, the northeastern corner.

Sandy cooks salmon caught by a friend on the Maine coast, adds salad and roasted yellow squash from the garden. She and beau Peter talk numbers:

> 23 households, 50 people, a span of seventy years between youngest
>
> and oldest, 3 apartments, 6 duplexes, 8 single homes, 270 acres of forest, pasture, and agriculture, 12 community meetings and 12 community work days annually, monthly committee meetings, 55 Jersey cows, 1 Holstein,
>
> the 4 Norwegian Fjord horses, 50 chickens, 240,000 honey-bees,
>
> 17,000 lbs. of cheese made each year, 26 varieties of vegetables grown,
>
> 425 lbs. of shiitake mushrooms harvested each summer, 50 cords of wood stacked (twice) to keep houses toasty, 2 outdoor wood-fired brick ovens,
>
> 1 sauna, 4 people who work at Dartmouth, 3 healthcare workers,
>
> 3 cheesemakers, 2 farmers, 2 executive directors, 1 teacher, 1 periodontist,
>
> 1 retired pharmacist, 1 forester, 1 craniosacral therapist, 1 state legislator, gardeners, scientists, several non-profit employees, small business owners,
>
> 450 gallons of maple syrup boiled each year, 7 dogs, 12 cats, 3 bunnies,
>
> many goldfish, 128 bird species sharing the woods, and more.

When I ask how much turnover there is, about one family each year decides to move on. Circumstances change, children get older. Some tire of the incessant "processing" required to live together. But the communal rewards are rich. It reminds me of America. If only I could learn how to live here.

> *Even the gnats know*
> *there's no place*
> *like home*

We leave Cobb Hill CoHousing and breakfast at Hartland Diner, a unique food experience crammed into a smallish room with an inner ring of classic counter seats, a handful of booths along the walls. Every inch crammed with memorabilia, theater posters, full-size cutouts of Bernie Sanders, Obama, Dr. Fauci, and more, more, more. We squeeze into the two vacant counter seats available and order breakfast, which come in large portions that are too much to finish. What a delight.

The *Hartland Diner Mission Statement* is laminated in color on both sides, tucked between the salt, pepper, and ketchup at each place setting. The brainchild of owner, head waitress, short order cook, bill payer, social media maven, hype-creator, hysteria junkie, is Mad Genius Nicole Bartner. She opened the diner at the age of 45 after "a long, nonlinear, varied career: getting certified to teach Elementary and Middle School English and Social Studies; working in a coffee shop; going to Law School; clerking for an Appellate Court Judge; working in a café; practicing Law serving as Editor in Chief AND in-house counsel for denofgeek.com before deciding she was not cut out to work for anyone else again in this lifetime..." Her crisp rant continues on the back page:

> The Hartland Diner is not just a diner. It's a Vermont Diner and THIS is what we're about:
>
> We are local. We work in a small town diner in small town Vermont because we value community and people and VERMONT. We believe we get more than we give by staying here, in Hartland, cooking for our friends and neighbors. And of course, we love food... [it goes on like this for a spell].
>
> What are we about? We are about Justice and Inclusion and Fair Wages paid for Honest Work in a safe and empowering workplace and The Vibe. Can you feel it?

The large world is filled with small places. Everyone wants a home. Sometimes you just dig in, create a vibe, make sure the coffee is rich, the eggs fluffy, the bacon from cows that roam free till the end.

> *A coffee cup half empty*
> *or half full*
> *on the counter*

Kennebunkport, Maine in Autumn. Sunny morning, cold, beautiful. Linda up early to take a long walk round the point. I wake with a headache I can't shake, but muddle through. Covid tests negative. Travel, in this modern endemic viral era.

I read Zadie Smith's *Intimations* at breakfast, her collection of pandemic essays, remember how the entire world was held hostage by invisible invaders. And how, though the worst of it is over, we're still susceptible to recurrences and paranoias of new viral hordes and ever-clever variants.

Zadie's chapter entitled "Suffering Like Mel Gibson" is a meditation on the invisible layers of pain that can be difficult to diagnosis when clouded by labels of "oppression," "privilege," and other sure judgments. Some people kill themselves over this very invisibility, she says, the seeming insignificance a veil.

Yet some judgments are sure in their very intensity, which I am reminded of this morning by news from Gaza. The war, sprung suddenly again yet nurtured for millennia. And I am relegated to my unspectacular personal complaints while on vacation in Kennebunkport, where the Bush clan still has a vacation home for the oil rich family of two presidents; relegated to the regrets of the privileged powerless to ease tragedies nurtured by generations, relentlessly. It is a strangely complicit seat assignment in the horror-comedy-opera of the daily news.

We finally load the car, drive to a lonely lighthouse Linda is intent on seeing despite its treacherous location nearly a mile's walk over jagged stone blocks. I turn back halfway, deterred by wind, spray, my cold, meet Linda back at the car after. The lighthouse, she said, was closed and there was nothing to see but the sea itself. A storm in the distance, approaching. And beauty everywhere.

The lighthouse waits
for ignition

HOME AGAIN. SLEPT WELL IN MY OWN BED. Linda at a forest refuge retreat, still in Maine. The house is mine for the day, till my grandson and his buddy come later in the week for a wild rumpus.

It is a strange calling, this contemplative life. An empty house and a full one, each a kind of Eden. I suspect the banned Tree of Knowledge is secretly the Tree of Life itself, at least that's what the boys seem to reveal in each tumble, query, spat. Keeping things lively. I find Bertolt Brecht's lines from "The First Psalm" in Bly's anthology:

> 7. We are travelling with tremendous speed toward a star in the Milky Way. A great repose is visible on the face of the earth. My heart's a little fast. Otherwise everything's fine.

That about sums up this return from pilgrimage, along with these lines from Tao Yuan-ming's "Two Drinking Songs":

> Wandering drunk in this beauty, who cares about my sorrows.
> I have left excitement behind, and what is not done...
> I walk around my study shouting and proud
> Because I can take up this life again.

This edge of continent on a great ocean, facing the Pacific Rim where tectonic plates, centuries and cultures keep crashing into each other, making a life, together.

> Bark of the great sea
> lions lounging, waiting
> for tide

Acknowledgements

It is good to have company on the journey. My hope is that any reader might become intrigued by the original sources in this book. In this spirit, I follow the best community practices outlined below.

From Code of Best Practices in Fair Use for Poetry:

> *Criticism, Comment, Illustration*
>
> *Poetic quotations are frequently employed by writers and artists in other disciplines. Perhaps the most non-controversial example is that in which a scholar, critic, or reviewer quotes from a poem in order to make a point about the poet in question or about his or her work. Because poetry arises out of and speaks to the particular circumstances (social, cultural, economic) of its writing, members of the poetry community were also united in their opinion that scholars and creators in other fields should be entitled to use apt selections of poetry for purposes other than criticism. Thus, they were supportive of quotation both for textual "illustration" and in the practice of visual artists who take inspiration from poetic works.*
>
> PRINCIPLE: *Under fair use, a critic discussing a published poem or body of poetry may quote freely as justified by the critical purpose; likewise, a commentator may quote to exemplify or illuminate a cultural/historical phenomenon, and a visual artist may incorporate relevant quotations into his or her work.*

Books may appear to spring from the Void immaculate, but they are birthed in unique eras, geographies, family constellations, and communal bonds. As always, much gratitude to my family for supporting this strange habit of writing, the nest from which all these words come. To my Emerald Street Writers clan, who gave me the initial encouragement to explore this contemporary *haibun* form of contemplative travelogue. To Saddle Road Press and, specifically, Ruth and Don for catching the vision of *Deep Travel* and enthusiastically bringing it into the world.

Many thanks to the Pacific Zen Institute for its encouragement of the arts in Zen practice. To Basho for his original inspiration. To modern expositors of *haibun* and *haiku*, whose online commentary is freely available on the web. And to this web of family, countries, language, and poetics that inform life on this planet.

About the Author

Dane Cervine is the author of many books of poetry, essays, memoir, and Zen meditations. He is a member of Sixteen Rivers Press in San Francisco, and the Emerald Street Writers in Santa Cruz, California—where he lives and works as a therapist [when not grandparenting, or traveling the world].

Dane Cervine's recent books of poetry include *The World Is God's Language* (Sixteen Rivers Press), *Earth Is a Fickle Dancer* (Main Street Rag), and *The Gateless Gate – Polishing the Moon Sword* (Saddle Road Press). Dane's poems have won awards from Adrienne Rich, Tony Hoagland, the *Atlanta Review*, *Caesura*, and been nominated for multiple Pushcarts. His work appears in *The SUN*, the *Hudson Review*, *TriQuarterly*, *Poetry Flash*, *Catamaran*, *Miramar*, *Rattle*, *Sycamore Review*, *Pedestal Magazine*, among others. Visit his website at: danecervine.typepad.com

[Or just search the Web for "Dane Cervine Writes"]

Printed in the USA
CPSIA information can be obtained
at www.ICGtesting.com
LVHW040424200924
791567LV00008BA/152

9 798990 054349